Joshua Uzoigwe:
Memoirs of a Nigerian
Composer-ethnomusicologist

Godwin Sadoh

ISBN: 1-4196-7380-7
ISBN-13: 978-1419673801

BookSurge Publishing
7290 B Investment Drive
Charleston, SC 29418
866.308.6235

To purchase additional copies of this book, please
visit www.amazon.com or www.booksurge.com

Acknowledgments

I am very grateful to several people who helped me in writing the very first book on the life and music of one of the famous twentieth century Nigerian composers, Joshua Uzoigwe (1946-2005). These people include Akin Euba, Nathan Davis, Deane Root, Renee Lysloff, Eric Moe, and Mathew Rosenblum.

This book is specially dedicated to the memory of my late mother, Taiwo Akinsanya, who prayed and desired that one of her children would become a professional musician. Her encouraging words and prayers will continue to stimulate my creative, scholarly and performance impulses.

To the memory of **Taiwo Akinsanya**

TABLE OF CONTENTS

LIST OF FIGURES

LIST OF TABLES

CHAPTER 1

INTRODUCTION

Objectives

This study is concerned with the life and works of Joshua Uzoigwe, a Nigerian composer and scholar. It examines the socio-cultural factors that most influenced his creative thought, inspiration and imagination. Uzoigwe's life and work explicate the imprint of both Western and Nigerian musical idioms in the works. His music is a vivid example of a modern intercultural work. The objectives may be summarized as follows:

1. To present a brief historical overview of contemporary Nigerian art music and the impact of European missionization and colonization. The background to the emergence of African art music is discussed in chapter 2.

2. To contribute toward the understanding of contemporary Nigerian art music, as manifest in the life of the composer Joshua Uzoigwe. The biography of Uzoigwe in chapter 3 illustrates the legacy of Western hegemony in post colonial Nigeria.

1

3. To discuss the stylistic features of Uzoigwe's music and the relationship between traditional and contemporary musical processes in African art music through examination of rhythmic, melodic and harmonic structures. The analysis of Uzoigwe's music is presented in chapter 4.

Significance of the Study

The significance of the study is threefold: (1) For Nigerians especially, and all scholars generally, it is important to document and study the life and works of notable composers like Joshua Uzoigwe. (2) The analysis of Uzoigwe's works can be source material for creative use by other composers in Nigeria, and throughout the world. The investigation thus affords Africans and non-Africans alike an opportunity to understand the creative procedures of contemporary African art music. (3) Finally, this study contributes toward ethnomusicological research on contemporary intercultural music.

State of Research

Studies in African art music have focused on documenting the lives and works of contemporary African composers (Uzoigwe 1978; Achinivu 1979; Alaja-Browne 1981; Bateye 1982). The literature on African art music is very brief. In most of the literature, there is an emphasis on discussing the musical language of the composers and the syncretic technique of their works. Discussion on the influence of ethnomusicology on neo-African music has been very brief at best. The works mentioned below are some of the most representative literature related to African art music.

Afolabi Alaja-Browne (1995) is one of the few scholars who have examined the imprint of European missionization on African art music. Akin Euba (1993) gives a brief description of colonization and the emergence of African art music.

Akin Euba (1970, 1988, 1989, 1992) and Kwabena Nketia (1982, 1994, 1995) emphasize the importance of adopting traditional creative principles and resources in contemporary African works. Nketia maintains that contemporary African composers can draw on distinctive features of African music that appeal to them as creative models. Euba takes the same position as Nketia and further suggests that contemporary composers should seek traditional resources for expression in their work. Other scholars like Kofi Agawu (1984) and Samha El-Kholy (1980, 1994, 1995) have also explored this theme.

Mosunmola Omibiyi (1989, 1992) has been able to identify some of the problems associated with music education in Africa. She gives a brief historical background to the emergence of African art music and the educational background of its practitioners and the intended audience. The influence of past colonial policies on the present educational system has yet to be examined. Music education is crucial to this topic because the mission schools were some of the institutions at which Africans were introduced to Western art music.

In light of the foregoing, we can see that African musicologists[1] have focused on several important issues in contemporary African art music. African art music can be viewed today as a nationalistic response to colonial legacy. In other words, what African music means to Africans is different now than what it meant to them in the past.

The role of nationalism and events that led to its emanation is of utmost importance to the emergence of African art music. Various political and socio-economic upheavals ignited the thinking and creative psyche of African artists, composers, performers, sculptors, painters and playwrights. In *Nigeria: Background to Nationalism* James Coleman (1958) argues that 1952 was the year when the nationalist movement became formally structured as a set of ideological parties functioning within a political system of a yet-to-be independent Nigeria.[2] Coleman makes reference to early resistance and protest movements among Nigerians that created a self-governing nation. He gives account of early militant resistance by Delta rulers such as the famous King JaJa against European penetration of the interior; the defiance of King Kosoko of Lagos and of the Sultan of Sokoto; and the Aba women's riots in eastern Nigeria in the late 1920's.

---

[1] By African musicologists, I mean active, indigenous scholars who are formally trained in ethnomusicology or historical musicology and who have been researching the music of Africa and publishing in scholarly journals.
[2] Nigeria became an independent nation in 1960.

Although Coleman's book on the political history of modern Nigeria never discusses music or art as such, he does point out some cultural and political occurrences that must have shaped the thinking of Nigerian composers generally. He distinguishes between traditional and modern nationalism. Traditional nationalism includes movements of resistance to the initial British penetration and occupation, early revolts provoked by the imposition or operation of alien political or economic coercions, and nativistic or messianic movements that provided psychological or emotional outlets for the tensions and frustrations produced by rapid cultural change. All these were as intensely nationalistic and anti-European as subsequent movements.

Modern nationalism, in Coleman's view, includes sentiments, activities, and organizational developments aimed explicitly at the self-government and independence of Nigeria as a nation-state existing on a basis of equality in an international state system. Modern African composers operate within the domain of modern nationalism. Through syncretism, they aspire for international recognition and at the same time maintain a local audience. Moreover, if they adhered to traditional nationalism, they would perform exclusively African traditional music.

Elizabeth Isichei (1983) in *A History of Nigeria*, further elucidates the impact of several political movements involving women and civil servants against colonialism and toward a self-determined state. Her book covers both political and church history in Nigeria. Indeed,

Nigerian church history cannot be separated from the development of African art music. Isichei observes that the movements decried colonialism in general, administrative oppression and economic injustice in particular. Isichei includes the Christian church as one form of opposition. According to her, the African churches were founded in Lagos in the 1890's, for the most part, as breakaway movements from the older missionary churches. They were founded in a spirit of ecclesiastical nationalism, by educated Nigerians, resentful of continuing white domination.

Other scholars like Don Ohadike (1991), Adamu Mohammed Fika (1978), Richard Dusgate (1985), and Ade Ajayi (1965) have also discussed the issue of Africans' resistance to white domination in the light of political, economical, and socio-religious governance. Virtually every African society resisted European colonialism, confirming that Africans despise foreign domination. For various reasons, however, certain resistance movements have been of special interest to African nationalists and historians.

Although Nigerian nationalists fought for emancipation from external domination, paradoxically, truly indigenous culture was not realised. The aftermath has been an ambivalent and diffused culture. In other words, the society is bi-cultural--the alloy of traditional African and Western culture. Wole Soyinka and LeRoi Jones (1983) in *Theater and Nationalism* notes one of the crucial dilemma of the nationalists in Nigeria. According to Soyinka, most Nigerian nationalists were not cultural nativists; rather, they were eclectics, desiring to keep what was useful and attractive in the old (Nigerian) and fuse it with the new (Western). In their desire to forget colonialism and build a new Nigeria, they insisted on the necessity for a cultural synthesis of Western and indigenous elements. In other words, they strove to legitimatize their own indigenous culture and reinterpret it through Western idioms. Soyinka's idea of cultural nativist differs from Coleman's view of modern nationalism. A cultural nativist will mean a Nigerian artist who creates mainly traditional works without any Western influence. Whereas Coleman's intellection of modern nationalism is the syncretization of Western and Nigerian cultural values.

While early resistance to colonialism by Africans was an outright rejection of European domination and cultural values, modern Africans encourage a coexistence of the two cultures. The work of contemporary African composers typifies this ideation.

European missionaries, African and non-African musicologists document how African church organists and choirmasters began to write indigenous church hymns based on traditional sources. The experimental procedures include the use of African traditional instruments as accompaniment for singing. Dancing is initiated through the use of drumming. E. E. Lurry (1956), E. G. Parrinder (1956), Jacqueline Schaffer (1956), Johan Louw (1956), K. Carrol (1956), Kwabena Nketia (1958), and Akin Euba (1989) vividly describe the contribution of African culture to church music.

Methodology

The models for this study are Joshua Uzoigwe's book, *Akin Euba: An Introduction to the Life and Music of a Nigerian Composer*, and Afolabi Alaja-Browne's M.A. thesis, "Ayo Bankole: His Life and Works." Uzoigwe's book illustrates how a bi-cultural creative mind copes with the challenge of harmonizing two different cultural idioms, the African and the Western. He demonstrates how Euba's research on Yoruba drumming has influenced his compositions. Alaja-Browne's thesis reveals how Ayo Bankole's background in church music, Yoruba music (including Yoruba language) and Western music influenced his style of music. The two books both served as a secondary source of information and as a model for the study of the life and music of the modern African art music composer.

The research for the study was based on (1) one personal interview, (2) analysis of scores and audio recordings of Uzoigwe's compositions, and (3) information compiled from various published and unpublished written sources. I had one long interview with Joshua Uzoigwe himself on August 4, 1991, at the Obafemi Awolowo University, Ile-Ife, Nigeria. The interview was based on a thirty-five-point questionnaire given to Uzoigwe about one week earlier in order to prepare him for our meeting.

First, Uzoigwe provided me with a detailed history of his life from childhood to 1991. Second, he took time to clarify and expound on some of the preliminary conceptions I had formulated about his music. Through the help and influence of Professor Akin Euba, I was able to obtain photostat copies of the scores of Uzoigwe's music from Iwalewa-Haus, University of Bayreuth, Germany. Uzoigwe provided me with recordings of his music. I have performed some of his piano and vocal works in order to comprehend the complex and subtle structures of the music.

The major influence on my analytical methodology has been category and feature analysis as undertaken by Jan LaRue and described by Ian Bent in his book *Analysis* (1987:93-95). In both, structure is one of the aspects brought under examination. Consequently, the theory has been useful as methods to reveal Uzoigwe's style of composition. The theory was used in two ways. First, to examine the features of individual works, and second, to present an overview of the features in chapter four.

Category analysis breaks music into its component characteristics in order to illuminate its stylistic traits. The analysis of Uzoigwe's music is structured into twelve categories--tonal organization, harmonic organization, thematic process, cadences, rhythmic organization, texture, form, tempo and meter, dynamics, interrelations of music and dance, instrumentation and titles of works. Under each categories are discussions of specific features of Uzoigwe's music. This is done in order to compare his compositional devices and to give an overview of his creative style. Because a detailed structural analysis of Uzoigwe's works is outside the objective of this study, I have focused on the elements from the two cultures, African and Western, that have influenced his music.

CHAPTER 2

HISTORICAL AND SOCIAL BACKGROUND OF
MODERN AFRICAN ART MUSIC

The history of modern African art music is made up of several interwoven threads. The establishment of the Christian church in Africa during the nineteenth century is a turning point of Western musical influence. However, other institutions like the Christian mission schools, institutions of higher learning, the modern African elite, and the service bands also introduced Western music to Africans. Social, political, and economic factors had an integral role in establishing Western music in Africa.

The Church

The European Christian missionization that penetrated Africa as early as the fourth century A.D. (Nketia 1974:15) became more pronounced during the first half of the nineteenth century and brought about profound socio-cultural change. The impact of the Christian church on African art music cannot be ignored. Indeed, Africans were first exposed to Western music such as hymns, church anthems (both involve four part singing), and instruments (organ and/or harmonium) through the church. However, this exposure was at the expense of indigenous music. Through the church, Africans were taught to emulate European music as an ideal art form. Followers of the faith were prohibited from all forms of traditional

11

practices including the playing of traditional musical instruments both in and outside the church. The church missionaries feared that traditional music would lead people back to traditional religious practices. However, Western music was not easily incorporated because members of the congregation had no knowledge of the foreign language. Consequently, they had difficulty in singing hymns in a foreign language. Recognizing such problems, some European missionaries (with the help of the educated members of their congregations) translated European texts into indigenous languages. This effort represents the first attempt of adapting the Christian worship to traditional practices.

The effort to make Christian religious songs attractive to native converts merely introduced additional difficulties and was opposed by the more educated members of the congregation. The elite of the church opposed this effort because of the discrepancy between local dialects and European hymn tunes. Most African languages are tonal and, therefore, the meaning of a particular word depends on its intonation. In traditional culture, melodies mirror the tonal inflections of the song texts. When indigenous words are sung to precomposed European hymn tunes, the tunes invariably conflict with the tonal inflections of the words and distort their meaning.

The second level of adaptation was the introduction of parodied songs. At this level, sacred religious texts from the Christian Bible were juxtaposed with preexisting traditional materials or folktunes. Adolphus Turkson describes how the early Methodist church in

Ghana was losing members as a result of the prohibition of African music at worship. In order to attract the converts back, the missionaries had to encourage worshippers to replace the secular texts of *adenkum*[1] and *asafo*[2] songs with Christian religious texts from the Bible and to use these adaptions in the church. For instance, the names of traditional divinities were replaced with the name of God or Jesus. These songs became popular among the congregation because the texts and melodies were indigenous (Turkson 1992:67-68). The texts were indigenous because they were in local dialects.

There were other reasons why translated hymns were problematic for the churches in Africa. Western songs are based upon the underlying rhythms of European languages. As Akin Euba argues (1989:48), the concept of rhythm in Nigerian vocal music is different from that of Europe where poetic meter is important. Therefore, African texts are not appropriate to European tunes.

Moreover, European church hymns alienated the African church congregations, because they were unsuitable for dancing. This was due to the prohibition of traditional musical instruments, which could have provided the natural rhythmic background for movement. Turkson argues that the whole structure of the performing arts was paralyzed when early missionaries banned drumming and dancing from the church.

---

[1] *Adenkum* is a musical type performed by older Fante women as recreational music (see Turkson 1992:66).
[2] *Asafo* is the music of warrior associations in Ghana (ibid:68).

He explains that the different components of the performing arts in Africa are so interwoven that subtracting one paralyzes the structure of the whole, and the remainder cannot perform as efficiently (Turkson 1992:78).

Experiments with translated church hymns continued to dissatisfy the educated elite in the church congregation, including the church organists and choirmasters. Therefore, African church musicians began to write their own hymns. Experimental composition included adapting existing indigenous melodies to newly composed local texts. In other instances, the composers created new tunes for newly composed indigenous texts. This involved creating melodies with contours that followed the tonal inflections of the words. Thus, the texts retained their proper meaning when sung. An in-depth study of the relationship between tonal language and melodic contour falls outside of the scope of this study and has already been undertaken by scholars like Ademola Adegbite (1974), Kofi Agawu (1984), Afolabi Alaja-Browne (1981), Lazarus Ekwueme (1974), and Akin Euba (1989).

According to Afolabi Alaja-Browne, Nigerian musicians began to compose their own church hymns using indigenous languages around 1902 (Alaja-Browne 1981:4). There is a record of similar development in other parts of Africa as shown by A. M. Jones (1976) in South Africa, Canon E. E. Lurry (1956) in Uganda, E. G. Parrinder (1956) in West Africa, Jacqueline Schaffer (1956) in Central Africa, and Johan Louw (1956) in Malawi. Notable pioneering church

organists and choirmasters in Nigeria were Dr. Thomas Ekundayo
Philips (1884-1969), Rev. J. J. Ransome-Kuti (1885-1930), Mr. T. A.
Bankole (1900-1977), Harcourt Whyte (b. 1905), and Ephraim Amu
(1899-1995) of Ghana.

The newly created church hymns retained some European musical
elements but also incorporated African elements. For instance, the
hymn writers used the Western diatonic scale and organ or
harmonium accompaniment. It was these experimental procedures
in the church that marked the beginning of the syncretization of
traditional African and Western music. Consequently, we could argue
that the development of African art music is rooted in the efforts of
the pioneering African church organists and choirmasters. These
early composers subsequently created advanced works such as
church anthems, sacred cantatas and oratorios.

The Africanization of the Christian church is more profound in the
so-called Aladura churches found in different parts of the continent.
The emergence of the Aladura churches (prayer churches) stems
from the disastrous influenza epidemic that invaded West Africa in
1918. African dissatisfaction with the failure of the established
churches to help them led to the formation of prayer groups that
followed a path of their own, until the deviations were such that the
prayer groups were forced to part company with the Anglican
Church and establish their own worship in 1922.

The new emphasis reflected both the African belief in prayer and spiritual healing, and the influence of literature emanating from a pentecostal church known as Faith Tabernacle in Philadelphia in the United States (Turner 1967:3).

One link to African traditional religion in the Aladura doctrine is the way in which the witch is seen as the personification of evil; thus, purification and liberation from witchcraft is emphasized (Isichei 1983:463). Another form of adaptation of traditional practices in the Aladura churches is the incorporation of handclapping and swaying dance movements. The use of drums and other traditional instruments in the Aladura churches--for example, the celestial Church of Christ, the Cherubim and Seraphim Church, and the Christ Apostolic Church--further strengthened the Africanness of the music. Thus, the congregation has been able to appreciate this type of music because its roots lie in more familiar traditional culture.

Christian Mission Schools

The music curriculum prepared by the missionaries in Christian schools was another strategic scheme for imposing Western musical values on Africans. This view is shared by Mosunmola Omibiyi who writes, "The aim was merely to produce catechists, priests and headmasters who could read music, and play hymns and chants on the harmonium from staff notation . . . . The content of the curriculum was confined to singing, rudiments of music and harmonium playing" (Omibiyi 1989: 29).

Apparently, the intention of the missionaries in this case was to meet the immediate needs of the church.

Throughout elementary and secondary schools, African traditional music was excluded from the syllabi during the colonial era. Rather, the curriculum consisted of Christian hymns, European folksongs and songs with vernacular texts set to preexisting English folk melodies.[3] Special schools like government secondary schools--Queens' College and Kings' College, in Nigeria--added piano playing and the history of Western music to the syllabi. Students showing promising talents were enrolled for the Associated Board of the Royal Schools of Music, London, examinations.

Nketia noted the same trend in Ghana, then called the Gold Coast. The music curriculum of Western-style education introduced by the churches emphasized Western hymns, school music, and art music. At the Presbyterian Training College in Akropong, Ghana, a compilation of songs translated into Twi and arranged for male voices included excerpts from the works of Haydn, Bach, Beethoven, and Brahms. In 1933, the Education Department of the Gold Coast announced the introduction of the Associated Board of the Royal Schools of Music, London, examination. All music students were encouraged to take the examination because it was considered to be the best around (Nketia 1974:15).

---

[3] See also related articles by Mensah (1989) and Nketia (1995) which discuss the deliberate imperial policy that led to the institutionalization of Western art music in Africa.

Prior to the mid-1980's, the formal music syllabus in African schools included only European music. Thus, students who participated in art music while in school could graduate without any knowledge of their cultural heritage, but with a taste for Western life styles and music. Informally, schools had drumming and dancing ensembles that were based on traditional idioms. It was in the late 1980's that African music was first introduced into the Nigerian school syllabus by the Federal Ministry of Education. For the first time in the history of music education in Nigeria, pupils were being introduced to the music of their mother land. This new syllabus introduced both the study of traditional music in Nigeria and the study of modern African art music by African composers (Euba 1988:108). It was also about this time that the West African Examinations Council introduced a new syllabus for music in the prospectus of the West Africans' Schools' Certificate[4] (now called the General Certificate of Education).

Institutions of Higher Learning

In teacher training colleges,[5] which supplied most of the personnel for the Christian missions, the music curriculum comprised rudiments of Western music and harmonium playing. It is not

---

[4] West Africans' Schools' Certificate is the High School Diploma awarded to successful candidates after graduation.
[5] The teacher training colleges are one of the tertiary institutions between the high school and university. The diploma awarded at graduation is about two steps above high school diploma and about two steps below university first degree (B.A. degree).

surprising that educated Africans from such schools would deprecate their own music since they had not been exposed to it in school. At the university level, however, music was absent from the curriculum. Music was used, rather, as entertainment and as an extracurricular activity (Omibiyi 1989:30). Students at this level were exposed to music through the musical productions organized by music clubs within the university community.

Starting from about the 1960's, departments of music were introduced into Nigerian universities. Prominent among these are the departments of music at the University of Nigeria, Nsukka, the University of Lagos,[6] and the University of Ife (now Obafemi Awolowo University). A critical look at the current curricula of these institutions presently reveals the dominance of Western classical music over traditional music. The curricula consist of Western orchestration, history, counterpoint, harmony, and studies in Western instruments, particularly the piano and orchestral instruments. Performance minors or majors are made to study mostly works by Western European and American composers.

Bode Omojola (1995:167) observes that, until recently, the music curricula at both federal and state levels in Nigeria tended to focus mainly on the study of European music. Although efforts are now being made in institutions such as the Universities of Nigeria, Ife, Ilorin and The Polytechnic, Ibadan, to incorporate traditional music

---

[6] The Department of Music at the University of Lagos has been closed down since late 1980's.

in the curricula, the teaching of traditional Nigerian music has yet to take its rightful place within the educational system in the country. Omojola further explains that the teaching of traditional instruments tends to come and go as yearly budgets allow. For example, although traditional Igbo instrumental instructors were hired on a part-time basis to teach at the University of Nigeria in the 1977-78 session, they were not available in the 1978-79 and 1979-80 sessions. Thus, while the university recruited teachers both within and outside the country to teach European music on a regular basis, it did not consider the recruitment of instructors of traditional music as equally important. The same trend continues today.

The Modern African Elite

The word "elite" describes a small but powerful dominant group within a particular society. The modern elite of Africa is made up of a few Europeanized, educated, and politically and/or economically powerful Africans. Some of the people in this class have played a major role in the development and establishment of local contemporary art music. Though they may be few in numbers, members of such an elite can often be very influential both culturally and ideologically. In modern African society, one can observe various types of elite groups according to special interests: economics and business, cultural expression (the media and related institutions), sports, military, education, and various professions.

The origins of elitist taste in Africa can be traced to early slavery and missionary activities. Regarding the latter, the European missionaries intended to introduce Western civilization to Africa by stratifying the society into three groups: the lower class, middle class and wealthy (Ajayi 1965:1-23). A small segment of the society was chosen to be sent to European countries such as Britain to be trained in professional skills and thereby acquire the European custom. This segment of the society constituted the upper middle class and the affluent. The missionaries intended these Africans to return with European tastes and to reform the African masses into a European-style society. Thus, they were being used as instruments of social change: the Europeanization of Africa.

The other source of African elitism emerged from the slave returnees. According to Biodun Jeyifo, from about the 1860's concerts and other forms of Western-derived entertainment were presented in Lagos by members of a new African social elite made up of educated or professionally trained returnees (former slaves and their descendants) from Sierra Leone, Brazil and Cuba. The principal forms of entertainment were the variety concert and the operatic drama (Jeyifo 1985:41). Most of the returnees had some prestige and social status because of the Western education they had received. Thus, they were intermediaries between European and African culture.

As a result of the European taste they had acquired, the elite favored and nurtured European styles of music, particularly Western classical music. This was achieved by organizing regular public concerts and performing as instrumentalists or singers in them. Today, some of the Nigerian elite even have personal choirs that give regular concerts in private mansions. Those who do not have private singers regularly invite individual choral groups and instrumentalists to perform in their mansions at festive occasions like Christmas, Easter, and the new year.

As Margaret Peil has illustrated, elite music in the early twentieth century in Lagos was largely imported from Europe; R. A. Coker and Ekundayo Philips, the first Nigerian musicians trained in Europe, concentrated on oratorios and organ music for the churches (Peil 1991:126-127). Alaja-Browne discusses some of the early musical activities by the Nigerian elite. He writes that Rev. Coker was said to have trained a large number of Nigerian women in the performance of Western classical music between 1880 and 1890. Furthermore, he organized a number of public concerts known as the Coker concerts which became the center of social life in Lagos. Other notable Nigerians in the musical life of the nineteenth century were Agnes Richards, a contralto singer; Herbert Macaulay, an engineer and violinist; Dr. King, medical practitioner and musician; and Adolph Williams, a singer (Alaja-Browne 1995:80).

The activities of elitist organizations like the Musical Society of Nigeria (MUSON) have contributed immensely to the growth and nurturing of art music in Nigeria. Since its inception in 1983, MUSON has organized regular concerts of both Western and African art music in Lagos. The patrons and audiences of MUSON concerts are the cream of the Nigerian elite such as expatriates, international business men and women, members of the diplomatic corps, professionals and intellectuals. These people have a taste for art music and support its activities morally and financially. These men and women have laid the foundation for African art music through their musical activities. They have not only pioneered the art of public performance, but have particularly fostered the culture of European classical music in Nigerian society. Hence, these efforts have contributed immensely to a thorough Westernization of the African society.

The Service Bands

Another means of early contact with European music was the service bands of the army, police, and navy. These bands were established by the colonial administrations in various parts of Africa around the early nineteenth century (Nketia 1974:16). In Nigeria, all sectors of armed forces have schools of music where members of the bands receive formal training in music. From the start the curricula of such schools were predominantly Western-oriented until the latter part of the twentieth century.

Some of the musicians were even sent abroad periodically (especially to London) to receive intensive training in Western music. The performance repertoire of such bands included the works of Baroque and Romantic composers.

The realization of independence in 1960, coupled with the activities of the nationalist movements, inspired Nigerian military bands to start employing traditional source materials in their compositions. Prior to this time, they had been encouraged by the colonial officials to learn and perform exclusively European music. The best attempt to Africanize their repertoire is the arrangement of folk themes based on Western harmony for the orchestra.

Presently in Nigeria, a typical military orchestra consists of clarinets, trombones, trumpets, tubas, saxophones and other Western musical instruments. Traditional instruments may include rattles, wood clappers, and local drums. The colonial legacy in the Nigerian military is exemplified by a combination of more Western musical instruments and fewer indigenous instruments in the orchestra.

Kwabena Nketia describes how as far back as the 1830's Ghanaians were taught to play Western music to entertain those who lived in the European forts and castles (Nketia 1974:16). The need for providing Western musical entertainment for colonial officials and traders was met subsequently by the army and the police bands, to which Africans were recruited and trained by Western band conductors. The repertoire of the bands consisted mainly of popular

European tunes which the instrumentalists learned by ear. According to Nketia, before the attainment of independence, it was these bands that entertained people at the European clubs and played for the garden parties held by governors of the colonies.

The creation of military bands by the colonial officials was intended primarily for recreational purposes. The training of the musicians and the type of music they were made to perform represent one of the early contacts by Africans with Western music. The performance of European music helped in shaping the taste of the elite for Western culture. From the information given by Nketia, we can deduce that it is the upper middle class and the affluent that developed a taste for Western music.

Economic and Political Factors

Nketia and Euba write that Western instruments were introduced to Africa through trade with Europe. Before their commercialization Western instruments were found mainly in the church and in the military (Nketia 1974:14 and Euba 1993:4). The adoption of such popular instruments like the guitar and the piano by local musicians in most parts of Africa followed this trend of commercialization.

These developments were fostered and strengthened through the efforts of the Christian church and the colonial officials. The church and the colonialists worked closely together to eradicate traditional practices while promoting Western cultures and value systems.

However, the imposition of Western cultural values was restricted to certain parts of Africa. For instance, European life styles were not totally forced on northern Nigeria. The colonial policy partly excluded Christian missions and Western education from the Muslim emirates. Although the colonialists encouraged a literacy in Arabic characters (Isichei 1983:441), there were some Christian missions in the north such as the Sudan Interior Mission. Political and economic policies favored the flourishing of Western trade in Africa. Policies that favored local trade were to the advantage of European government.

Missionization, colonization and trade all combined in the Westernization of Africa. The missionaries' intention was not just to preach the gospel. They employed subtle means to impose Western civilization on Africa. Thus, Africans were made to deprecate their cultural heritage and look up to European cultural values as the ideal.

The voices of dissent from the African elite coupled with the activities of the nationalist movements in and outside the church inspired the revival of African traditions including music. However, experimental works by pioneering church organists and choirmasters produced compositions neither entirely African nor entirely Western. These works could be best understood as a synthesis of African and Western musical idioms. Thus, the syncretization of the two musical idioms started in the church.

Indeed, the historical sketch given above clearly suggests Western hegemony over African cultural values. Suffice it to state here that all colonial efforts were geared toward the Westernization of Africa. European values remain vividly manifest in modern African art music and its audience.

Today with the absence of colonization, contemporary Africa is part of on-going global transanction. With the standard of technological advancement, media, international monetary policies and global ideologies, Africa is exposed to cultural values and ideas from all over the world. Arjun Appadurai describes these global cultural flows as landscapes (1990: 6-11). Through media prints, internet facilities, record/cassette industries, and satellite systems (TV, video), modern African composers are daily exposed to new styles of musics from all over the world. As creative artists, they naturally respond to artistic phenomena coming from other cultures. The idea of appropriating Western musical idioms in their work is the result of the colonial experience. In the following chapters, I will explore the impact of African Westernization on the life and music of Joshua Uzoigwe. Uzoigwe's life typifies the experience of an average African which has been shaped by a bi-cultural environment.

CHAPTER 3

THE LIFE OF JOSHUA UZOIGWE

The Formative Years

Joshua Uzoigwe was born on July 1, 1946 in Umuahia, Imo State, in eastern Nigeria.[1] He belongs to the Igbo, one of the three major ethnic groups in Nigeria. Uzoigwe attributes his first contact with music to participation in various musical activities in his village. He sang as a child in a local choir and occasionally performed the works of Harcourt Whyte, including hymns and sacred anthems, during special church services. Whyte was one of the pioneers of indigenous church music compositions among the Igbo. The works of Whyte represent some of the earliest attempts at syncretizing Western and African musical idioms by church organists and choirmasters.

An individual's perception of the world is determined by accumulated past experiences. These experiences are very much modified by personal, even bodily, identification with surrounding human activity including music and physical movement (such as dance or wrestling in Igboland). All the musical events observed by Uzoigwe in his childhood influenced his over-all musical perception. His participation in local musical activities and events subsequently

---

[1] Information on the life history of Uzoigwe was obtained from a personal interview I had with him in 1991 at the Obafemi Awolowo University, Ile-Ife, Nigeria.

28

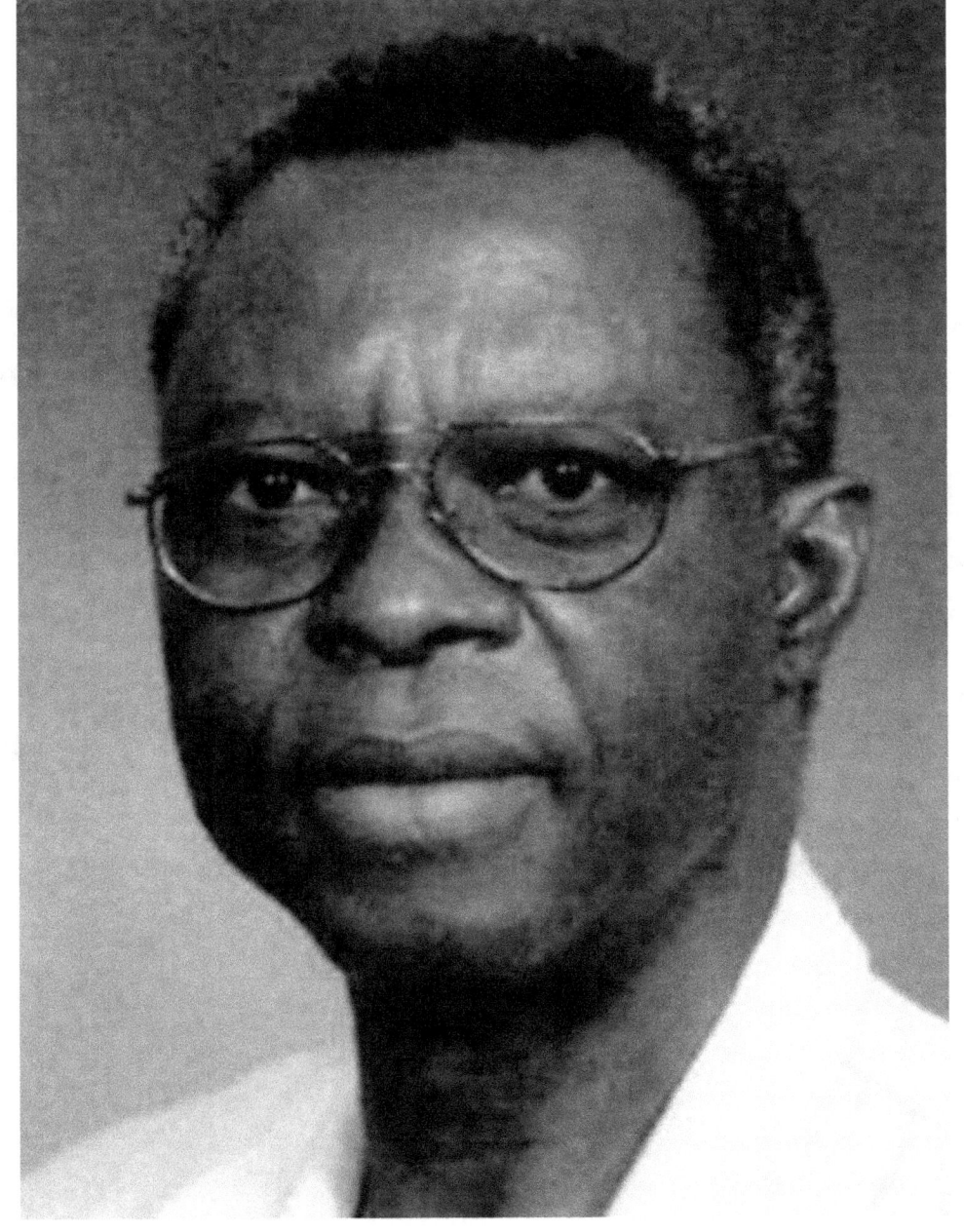

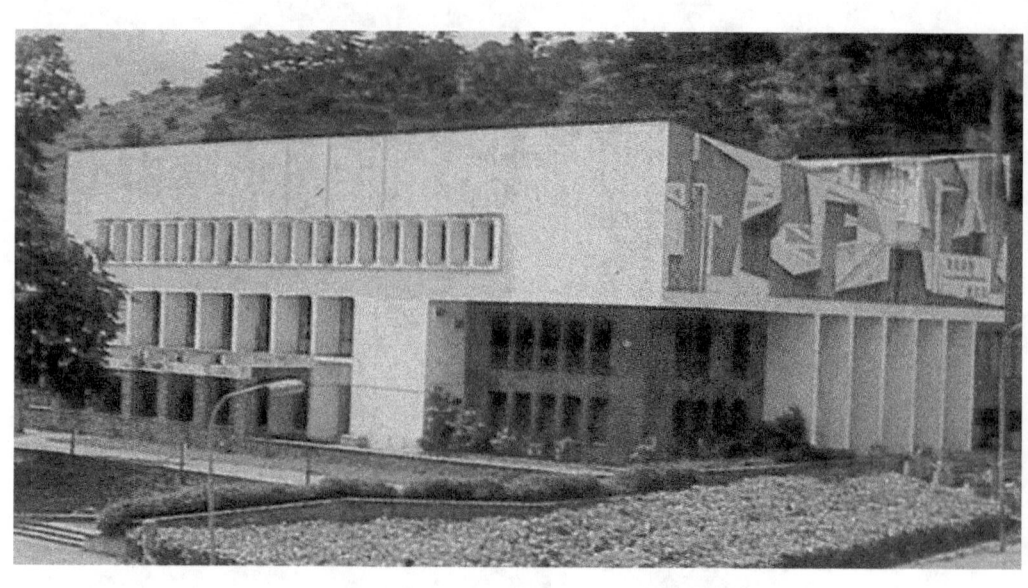

helped to inculcate in him indigenous African (particularly Igbo and Yoruba) values even while he was being exposed to Western music. As Meki Nzewi observes, creativity among the Igbo is deeply rooted in indigenous everyday socio-religious experience (Nzewi 1991:10). The annual wrestling match in Uzoigwe's community offered one forum for music performance. However, Uzoigwe was mainly involved in activities associated with audience participation such as clapping, singing and dancing. The wrestling bouts were always accompanied by *mgba* music. *Mgba* refers to a popular musical ensemble that accompanies wrestling in the southern part of Igboland (Uzoigwe 1986:60). In addition to his experience in the church, the young Uzoigwe was often exposed to traditional music such as this.

Young Uzoigwe, like many Africans, grew up bi-cultural and bi-musical. By "bi-cultural," I am referring to a cultural phenomenon analogous to bi-lingualism. Africans and Asians often find themselves living simultaneously in two different cultural worlds, modernized Western and traditional indigenous. Bi-culturalism is most pronounced in those regions once colonized by a Western power. Music, language, educational and political institutions, even food are more obvious manifestations of bi-culturalism. Bi-musicality refers specifically to the intuitive understanding of and/or trained skills in two or more musical traditions. In Uzoigwe's case, this refers to knowledge of both Western and indigenous musics. In other words, he has become equally comfortable with both European and African musical scales, rhythms, and structures.

Mantle Hood describes the Western musician who wishes to study Eastern (or African) music or the Eastern (including African) musician who is interested in Western music as facing the challenge of bi-musicality (Hood 1960:55). For illustration, Hood refers to the musicians of the Imperial Household in Tokyo as being bi-musical. The musicians have undergone strict training since childhood, not only in the *Gagaku* dances and instrumental techniques, but also in the performance of Western music of the classical period. In their capacity as official court musicians, they are required to perform both *Gagaku* and Western classical music. Bi-musicality is very crucial to the concept of modern African art music.

In 1960, Uzoigwe gained admission to Kings College in Lagos, one of the leading secondary schools in Nigeria. It was at King's College that he had his first formal lessons in Western music. The music curriculum included history, theory, and harmony of Western music. Apart from the music classes he took at school, Uzoigwe also received private piano lessons and performed mainly European pieces. Uzoigwe began exhibiting considerable musical talent in performance. Indeed, he won prizes during his first year and final year, including first prize in a piano competition. He also won another first prize with his partner in a piano duet competition.

Uzoigwe's involvement in religious and musical activities at Kings College played a part in his decision to make music a career. He belonged to the Protestant church and was also a member of the school choir. The major impact of missionization and colonialism on

Kings College could be observed in the singing and playing of European music in the school choir and at Sunday services. In the school the students were taught Western cultural values, thereby developing a taste for a European lifestyle. Kings College was built as a model school; however, it has attracted an unusually large number of children from wealthy and upper-middle-class families. The reason for this might be that members of the wealthy and the upper-middle-class moved in those social circles that enabled them to identify the best educational opportunities existing locally. For the European colonialists who conceived it, pupils were to be trained as future leaders of Nigeria. The intention of the colonialists was that these pupils would later in life become civil servants, intellectuals, business figures and politicians who could be exploited by the colonialist, as instruments of Western hegemony.

Professional Training

After graduating from the Kings' College, Uzoigwe studied music at the International School, Ibadan (1965-1967), and at the University of Nigeria, Nsukka[2] (1970-1973). Uzoigwe moved to the International School for two reasons--(1) It was one of the leading secondary schools in Lagos like the King's College, and (2) it was recommended to him by his former private music instructor, Major J. J. Allen, who was then a colonial administrator. While at the International School, he came to know and perform the works of

---

[2] University of Nigeria, Nsukka was the only one to offer music among the three or four universities existing in Nigeria at the time.

prominent Nigerian musicians who had been trained abroad. Some of these musicians include Fela Sowande (composer and organist), Ayo Bankole (composer and organist), Christopher Oyesiku (singer), and Akin Euba (African musicologist and composer). Through the study and performance of their works, Uzoigwe became exposed to compositional techniques of modern African art music, the devices that would later become the basis of his creative work. At the International School and the University of Nigeria, Uzoigwe studied orchestration and counterpoint, theory and history of European art music, and performance (piano and singing)--all completely Western in conception and orientation.

Uzoigwe's music career was interrupted by the Nigerian civil war from May 1967 to January 1970.[3]   The civil unrest and resistance to the Nigerian government in fact began on the campus of the University of Nigeria, Nsukka. The Igbo ethnic group led by an Ibo elite and military officer Chukwuemeka Odumegwu Ojukwu[4] felt cheated politically and economically by the two other dominant groups, particularly the Yoruba and the Hausa.

Recalling his experiences after the war, Ken Saro-Wiwa (a former popular playwright and renowned civil rights activist) describe how students and staff were being asked by Ojukwu and other sympathetic lecturers to volunteer for different services connected

---

[3] The Nigerian civil war started in 1967 and ended in 1970. It was a political war between the Federal Republic of Nigeria (Yoruba, Hausa and other minority ethnic groups) and the secessionist Biafra Republic.

[4] Chukwuemeka Odumegwu Ojukwu was the governor of the former East Central State of Nigeria at the time.

with the war, such as fire-fighting and Red Cross. University staff were asked to voluntarily contribute about five percent of their salaries to the war fund. Staff and students also volunteered for other forms of military training (Saro-Wiwa 1989:67). Rather than continuing his studies, Uzoigwe volunteered for military service in the Biafran Army. Biafra was the name of the nation of the breakaway Igbo group.

Uzoigwe began writing poems during the war as a way to express himself in the absence of musical instruments. After three years with little musical activity, his music career suffered some setbacks. For instance, the absence of a piano made it impossible for him to practice for three consecutive years and his skills in musical performance waned. He could not find a piano to practice because the University of Nigeria, Nsukka, was closed down during the war.

Uzoigwe's first major work, *Four Igbo Songs,* was written while he was still studying at Nsukka. They were inspired by the sonorous voice of Ori Enyi Okoro, a young Nigerian soprano and a fellow student at the Department of Music, University of Nigeria. In 1973, Uzoigwe received a scholarship from the government of the former East Central State of Nigeria to continue his music studies at the Guildhall School of Music, London. This opportunity arose as a result of the numerous concerts he had with Ori Okoro, for television programs and state events, as well as his earlier academic performance.

Uzoigwe studied piano and composition at the Guildhall School of Music from 1973 to 1977. Again, like schools he had attended in Nigeria, the Guildhall curriculum was entirely Western. He thus acquired a thorough training in European musical style, studying the works of his composition teacher and those of other contemporary African and Western composers such as Akin Euba, Arnold Schoenberg, Anton Webern and Alban Berg. Uzoigwe studied the works of African composers privately since they were not part of the curriculum of the Guildhall School of Music. The impact of this study on Uzoigwe will be seen in an analysis of his works (see chapter 4). As a student being trained in the Western tradition of art music, Uzoigwe's approach of studying the works of earlier composers is similar to that of Bach, Mozart, Brahms, Bartok and other Western composers in their formative years.

In 1976, at Guildhall School of Music, Uzoigwe wrote a work called *Two Songs* for Mixed Chorus. This was performed by the Contemporary Music Society, Guildhall School of Music, London, in the same year it was written. That same year, he wrote his first orchestral work *Nigerian Dances* for Chamber Orchestra, which was performed by the Contemporary Music Society, Guildhall School of Music, London, in 1976. Composing the *Dances* was encouraged by a Chinese friend who needed a contemporary piece to complete her repertoire for her final examination at the school. The *Dances* were later reduced for piano solo.

For the virtuoso pianists at the Guildhall School of Music, Uzoigwe wrote *Sketches* for piano in 1977. Similar to the piano music written by Ayo Bankole, who also studied at the Guildhall (1957-61), Uzoigwe's piano music at Guildhall shows the influence of the various styles he was exposed to. Before graduating from the school in 1977, Uzoigwe wrote an orchestral work entitled *Lustra Variations* for Symphony Orchestra. This work was his only work for full orchestra and was performed by the Guildhall School of Music and Drama Symphony Orchestra in London in 1977.

At the Guildhall School of Music, Uzoigwe not only received training to be a composer, but he also prepared to become a music scholar. In 1974, he wrote an article titled "Three Songs" in collaboration with Gary Weltz, published in the *African Arts* journal of the Center for African Studies, University of California, Los Angeles. "Three Songs" is a theoretical analysis of Uzoigwe's own *Four Igbo Songs.*

In 1976, Uzoigwe won the prize in a composition competition at the Guildhall School of Music with his *Nigerian Dances* for a Chamber Orchestra. After four years of studies at Guildhall, Uzoigwe received two professional diplomas in music, namely: Licentiate of the Guildhall School of Music (piano playing and teaching) 1974, and Graduate of the Guildhall School of Music (pianoforte/composition) 1977.

In 1977, Uzoigwe went to the Queen's University in Belfast, Ireland, to study ethnomusicology with John Blacking. He was sponsored by both the former East Central State government and the University of Ife (now Obafemi Awolowo University). While at Queen's, Uzoigwe was introduced to different musical cultures from many parts of the world and, as time went on, he acquired greater knowledge of African music. With a comparative view of different musics of the world, Uzoigwe could understand why the local musicians deliberately avoid certain musical elements and why they employ others wholeheartedly. The results of his discoveries were later utilized in Uzoigwe's compositions.

The search for a deeper knowledge of African traditional music led Uzoigwe to compose some works on an experimental level. In 1978, he wrote his first work at Belfast called *Ritual Procession* for African/European Orchestra. It was performed in 1980 by the Department of Music Chamber Orchestra, University of Belfast. This work also marked the beginning of a new style to be adopted by Uzoigwe, a synthesis of both African and Western musical elements. Although one might see traces of this style in his previous works, it was in the *Ritual Procession* that it became more apparent. In the same year, Uzoigwe composed *Oja* for Wind Quartet, performed in 1980 by the Department of Music Chamber Orchestra. Uzoigwe was not pretending to be Western as a result of his education. He grew up with two distinct cultures around him. Consequently, his compositions reflects these cultural traits.

In 1978, Uzoigwe wrote and published his second scholarly article, "Contemporary Techniques of Composition by African Composers: A Preliminary Investigation," in the International Folk Music Council Newsletter, United Kingdom chapter. Uzoigwe formulated some theoretical concepts in the article that he considered necessary for a truly African art music. He demonstrated in practical terms the validity of some of these theoretical concepts in his own musical works as well as those of other leading Nigerian composers such as Ayo Bankole and Akin Euba for several composers' workshops in Britain, Holland, and Bulgaria, as well as lectures and seminars at the University of Ife in Nigeria.

While carrying out his doctoral field research in Owerri, Nigeria, from 1979 to 1980, Uzoigwe composed another work called *Masquerade I and II* for iyaalu drum and Piano. This work is mainly improvisatory in nature. The work was performed on Nigerian Television Aba in 1979 by the artists Yemi Olaniyan (drum) and Uzoigwe (piano). That same year, Uzoigwe was appointed lecturer at the Department of Music, Alvan Ikoku College of Education in Owerri, Nigeria, where he stayed until 1980. Uzoigwe later went back to write his Ph.D. dissertation at the Queen's University in 1981. At the end of his sojourn at Queen's University in 1981, Uzoigwe left for Nigeria with two degrees: M.A. and Ph.D. in ethnomusicology.

Professional Career

In 1981, Uzoigwe was appointed lecturer at the Department of Music, Obafemi Awolowo University, in Ile-Ife. Following the year of his appointment, he married the Irish woman Joanne McGuckin in his town, Umuahia, in the Imo State of Nigeria.

At the Obafemi Awolowo University, Uzoigwe was a music educator, composer, performer and musicologist. He directed several musical concerts in which he featured his own works and works by other modern African composers. His intention was to create an awareness of this music in an intellectual environment such as Obafemi Awolowo University and in Nigeria at large. Uzoigwe also held several administrative posts, such as member of the Board of Postgraduate Studies in 1982 and the Board of Studies in the Faculty of Arts in 1983. Uzoigwe's research activities at the Obafemi Awolowo University consisted of (1) an in-depth analytical study of the creative techniques of modern African art music, (2) further research on his Ph.D. dissertation topic, the *ukom* music of the Igbo, and (3) research on other types of Igbo traditional music. (For a full listing of Uzoigwe's published articles see the Bibliography.)

In 1981, Uzoigwe wrote a new work called *Fanfare* for Brass Ensemble, performed in 1985 by the Nigerian Army Band in Lagos. This was followed by another orchestral work, *Watermaid* for Voice Solo and Orchestra, yet to be premiered because of the absence of a standard orchestra in Nigeria. Uzoigwe once had a brilliant student who was a good trombonist. His name is Festus Oviagwe and his skillfulness on the trombone inspired *A Sketch for Trombone.*

Uzoigwe's scholarly activities also included participating in scholarly conferences. For instance, in 1985, he attended a conference at the University of Sydney in Australia organized by the International Association for the History of Religions. That same year he was promoted to senior lecturer at the Obafemi Awolowo University. He left Obafemi Awolowo University in 1991 for the University of Nigeria, Nsukka, where he worked until 1995. Uzoigwe moved to the University of Uyo, Akwa Ibom State, Nigeria, in 1995 where he is currently an Associate Professor and Head of the Department of Music.

Uzoigwe's contribution to knowledge has been in the area of musicology with special emphasis on studies of composition and performance. For many years, he has conducted analytical studies of the ethnography of musical performance in Nigeria. His intention has been to develop a general theory of African music, based on an orderly and systematic analysis of the structure of music and its meaning to both performers and audiences. In the process, Uzoigwe proposed that music is a social fact and the organization of tones is the result of decision making by the individuals in society.[5] In other words, form in Igbo music is the resultant shape created by the musicians' moulding of their musical conceptions in conformity

---

[5] Uzoigwe's philosophy is derived from his curriculum vitae.

to the social-event structure with which the music and/or musical performance is associated. Consequently, each performance situation determines the technical approach to selecting and realizing musical ideas. This theory is similar to Victor Turner's view of anthropology of performance in which he postulates that the force of a social drama consists in its being an experience or sequence of experiences which significantly influences the form and function of cultural performative genres (Turner 1986:95).

Joshua Uzoigwe departed this world on October 15, 2005, and was buried in Umuahia, Imo State, on November 5, 2005. His wife, Joanne McGurkin, passed away at Ile-Ife, in 1990. Uzoigwe is survived by three children, Uzo, Nneka and Ejike.

CHAPTER 4

THE MUSIC OF JOSHUA UZOIGWE

Uzoigwe, both as a man and an artist, is rooted in two cultures, African and European. With respect to the latter, this is due to his exposure to the Western European system of education in Nigeria and in England. The sources of his tone imagery are to be found in the kinds of music he experienced as a child in his town at Umuahia, at Lagos and Ibadan, and when studying in England.

Worthy of note is his use of Africanization as a process for assimilating adopted foreign forms into the musical life of his society. One of the features of Uzoigwe's musical history is the co-existence of old and new forms and their corresponding musical practices as living arts in a contemporary Nigerian society. This re-affirms one of the basic tenets of African philosophy that the past is always here with us and the future is not remote from us.

Uzoigwe's works can be described as modern intercultural music in which African and Western musical elements are more or less co-dominant. His experiences in the two cultures have enabled him to create music which is indisputably a synthesis of the two. As Uzoigwe rightly puts it,

> Most of my works have been influenced by my analytical studies of the ethnography of musical performance in African societies. They therefore involve the utilization of traditional African elements and techniques, as well as

41

a positive assimilation of qualitative and useful foreign musical ideas and creative methodologies (Morton and Collins 1992:938).

This is a reflection of his personality as a creative artist. He had one aim, to capture and reinterpret the African essence in his works.

The works I discuss below are the most representative of Uzoigwe's creative output. It is not my objective to give a detailed structural analysis of Uzoigwe's works; rather, I focus on some of the African and Western features of his music, thereby, placing them in the perspective of modern African art music. I will discuss the most salient features of Uzoigwe's works: (1) tonal organization, (2) harmonic organization, (3) thematic process, (4) cadences, (5) rhythmic organization, (6) texture, (7) form, (8) tempo and meter, (9) dynamics, (10) interrelations of music and dance, (11) instrumentation, and (12) titles of works.

Tonal Organization

The music of Uzoigwe is based on various pitch languages. His music displays a variety of means of organizing pitches. This section will examine melodic intervals, melodic structures, scales and tonal centers, and vocal range.

Melodic Intervals

The most frequently used melodic intervals in Uzoigwe's music are seconds, thirds, fourths and fifths. These intervals are mostly found in his vocal and instrumental works. Out of the four intervallic structures, the melodic progressions feature mostly major seconds, minor thirds, and perfect fourths. For instance, in *Ite Etipia Etipia* (one of the *Four Igbo Songs*), minor third appears fifty four times, major second appears fourty four times and perfect fourth, thirty one times. Other intervals in the song are minor seconds which appear ten times, major third-thirteen times, perfect fifth-once, and major sixth-twice only. Uzoigwe's predilection for seconds, thirds and fourths can be traced to Igbo traditional music in which these intervallic structures are very common (Ekwueme 1980:91). In Uzoigwe's tonal works such as *Four Igbo Songs--Eriri Ngeringe, Uyaroma, Ite Etipia Etipia, Tuzu* (mezzo soprano and piano accompaniment), *Nigerian Dances* (piano), *Sirene Limits* (SATB) and *Watermaid* (bass solo and orchestra), the widest melodic leaps are fourths and fifths. Examples 1a and 1b are representative of the predominant intervallic structures in Uzoigwe's music.

Example 1a. Melodic Intervals in *Ite Etipia Etipia*
mm. 17-24

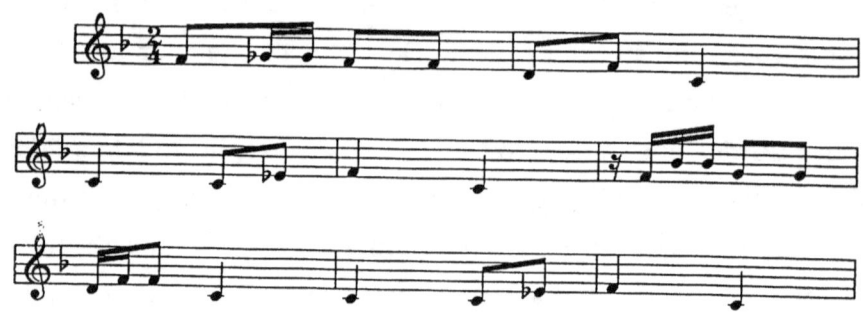

Example 1b. Melodic Intervals in *Nigerian Dances No.3*
mm. 5,6,12

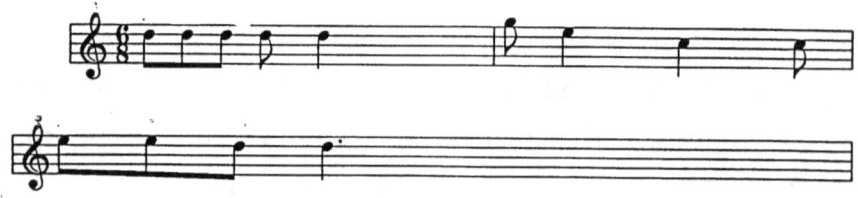

It is of interest to note in Uzoigwe's music that some intervallic structures are peculiarly found between specific pitches. As an illustration, major seconds are only seen between C and D, and between D and E in the principal theme of *Nigerian Dances No. 3*. In *Eriri Ngeringe*, minor thirds are only found between D and F, while in *Nigerian Dances No. 3,* between E and G. Perfect fourths are found mainly between G and C, and between C and F in *Uyaroma.* Example 2 shows major second between specific pitches in *Nigerian Dances No.3.* The restriction of certain intervals to specific pitches is the resultant effect of using melodic scales with short ranges. Thus, the limited notes make room for repetition between pitches.

Example 2. Short Intervals in *Nigerian Dances No.3*
m. 13

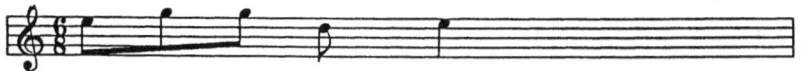

The atypical wide leaps of sixths, sevenths, octaves and ninths are mostly found in Uzoigwe's atonal music such as *Sketches For Piano* and *Oja[1]For Wind Quartet,* both of which are purely instrumental pieces. He employs wide leaps and make use of the whole keyboard instead of a confined range. Example 3 shows wide leaps in *Sketches For Piano.*

---

[1] *Oja* is the name of an Igbo flute, almost as ancient as the slit-drum in origin. It was made by early man of bird's bones. It has two holes and gives very penetrating shrill sounds. It is often used by the head of a work gang to encourage the labor (Mackay 1954:22).

Example 3. Wide Leaps in *Sketches For Piano No.1*
mm. 6,8,12

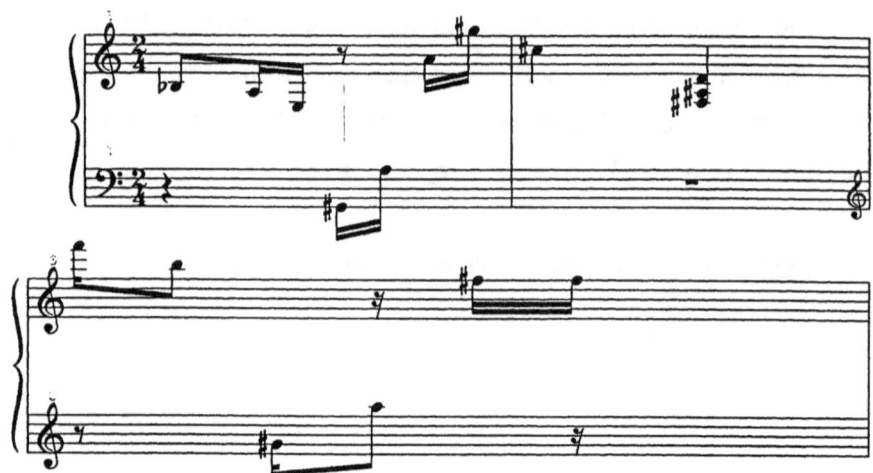

Melodic Structure

The melodic contour of Uzoigwe's music is determined by the intervallic structures of the pitches. Conjunct melodic shapes are commonly found in his vocal works, while the instrumental music is generally characterized by disjunct melodic shapes. The convention of using conjunct motion for vocal lines is implicit for the conjunct shapes of the vocal works. Another reason lies in the fact that some conventions are accustomed to vocal songs with small intervals as pleasing than the ones with wide leaps. Hence, the predominance of stepwise motion and thirds. The dexterity of instruments may account for the prevalence of more disjunct motion in his instrumental works. Examples 2 and 3 are representative of these two types of melodic contours.

Melodic motion in Uzoigwe's music usually starts from a high point and descends to a low point. The melodies of the *Four Igbo Songs* are traditional and as such conform to this technique since they were borrowed Igbo folk songs. This recalls Igbo traditional musical practices in which a descending pattern is the norm for musical melodies (Ekwueme 1980:105).[2] For instance, the 'singing' or melodic progressions of *ukom*[3] drumrow are always from the smaller keys--high point--to the larger ones--low point (Uzoigwe 1980:20). The downward melodic motion is present in both vocal and instrumental works of Uzoigwe. However, we must not overemphasize this point since there are a few instances in which the melodic motion starts from a low to a high point. Examples 4a to 4d shed light on descending melodic motion in Uzoigwe's music.

Example 4a. Descending melodic motion in *Uyaroma*
m. 4

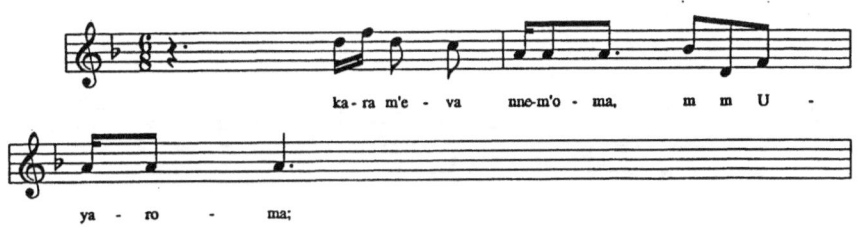

[2] This type of melodic motion is also observed in other African traditions (see Agawu 1984:50, 58).
[3] *Ukom* is an instrumental ensemble conceived principally as a symbolic accompaniment to the *okwukwu nwanyi* (women's burial) ceremony. It also has secondary use in the celebration of the Igbo New Yam festival, or the honoring of the Earth (*Ala*) Deity. The *ukom* drums has a fixed scale of ten tones (Uzoigwe 1986:53).

Example 4b. Descending melodic motion in *Ite Etipia Etipia*
m. 13

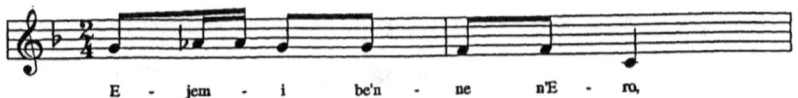

E - jem - i   be'n - ne   n'E - ro,

Example 4c. Descending melodic motion in *Nigerian Dances No.1*
mm. 7-10

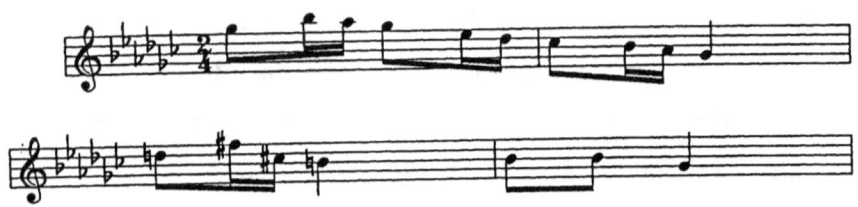

Example 4d. Descending melodic motion in *Sketches For Piano No.1*
m. 1

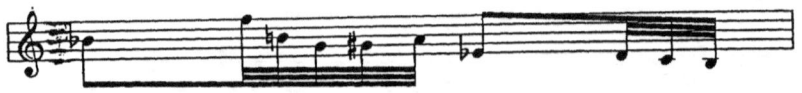

Another type of melodic shape found in Uzoigwe's music is the
antecedent and consequent phrases. This trait is observed in his
vocal and instrumental music. The two phrases becomes a *period*
when combined to form a larger structural unit in a question and

answer relationship. This technique is similar to the popular call-and- response singing in African music. As Meki Nzewi observes:

> The most significant structural feature of folktale songs is the invariable presence of a phraseal theme which recurs at equidistant points in the cycle of a melodic meter. This is the phrasing constant for a folktale song (Nzewi 1991:124).

In other words, the melodic phrase of Uzoigwe's songs is in two parts, a phrasing constant and the variable (narrative bearing) part. The variable section carries the textual development of the narrative. The fixed section, the phrasing constant, is usually syllabized. It gives metric unity to the form of the song. It also serves as a structuring referent which guides the temporal organization of the variable section. Its melodic-syllabic characteristics are often a vocal transformation of an instrumental idiom (ibid.). Agawu notes the occurrence of the two organizing principles in Ghanaian traditional music (Agawu 1984:45). See example 5 (Likewise see examples 4a to 4c for similar phrase structure). Notice the first and the second phrase combining to form a period.

Example 5. Two Phrase Structure in *Ite Etipia Etipia*
mm. 25-32

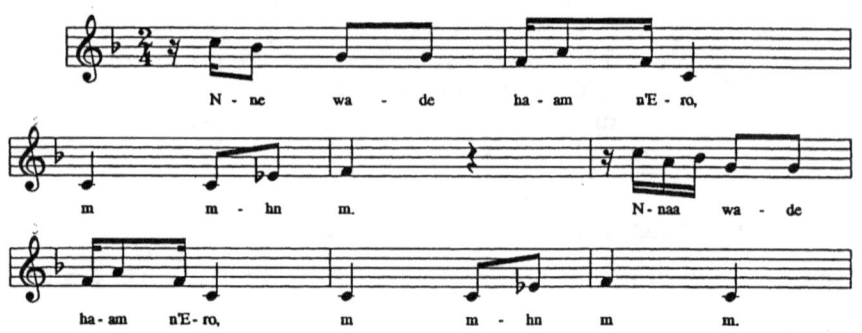

Scales and Tonal Centers

Uzoigwe uses different types of pitch collections such as tetratonic, pentatonic, hexatonic, heptatonic, octatonic, diatonic scales and the twelve tone row. The most commonly used ones are the anhemitonic pentatonic, hexatonic and the heptatonic scales. The three scales incorporate semitones and whole tone intervals. In African music where these scales are employed, the melodic progressions are restricted to small intervals such as seconds, thirds and fourths (Nketia 1974:152). This clarifies why melodic intervals in Uzoigwe's music are dominated by short leaps. One obvious reason for the frequent use of these scales in Uzoigwe's music can be traced to Igbo traditional music where they are often employed (Ekwueme 1980:105).

Uzoigwe uses these scale systems to evoke melodic and harmonic nuances of Igbo music in his works. See examples 6a to 6d for some of the common scales in Uzoigwe's music.

Example 6a. Pentatonic Scale in *Nigerian Dances No.2* mm. 46-65

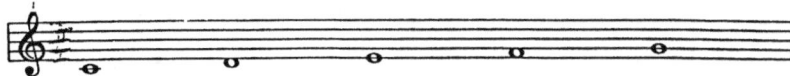

Example 6b. Hexatonic Scale in *Eriri Ngeringe*

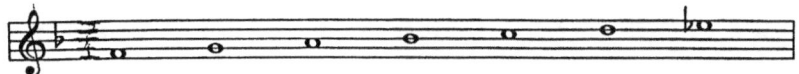

Example 6c. Heptatonic Scale in *Ite Etipia Etipia*

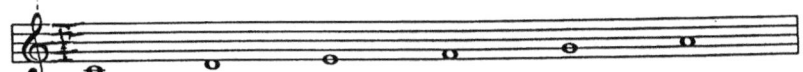

Example 6d. Octatonic Scale[4] in *Nigerian Dances No.3* mm. 57-84

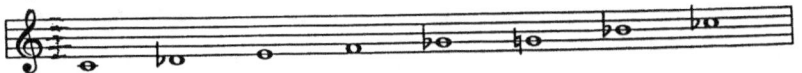

---

[4] Uzoigwe often creates his own type of scales for specific compositions. This example is representative of his own version of octatonic scale.

Uzoigwe began employing the twelve-tone technique while studying at the Guildhall School of Music, in London. He learned the technique through classroom assignments and by studying the works of Arnold Schoenberg and his two pupils, Alban Berg and Anton Webern. In one of my conversations with Uzoigwe, he explains that he often breaks the row into minute 'cells' and then shuffles them around to create a whole work. The use of twelve tone technique in Uzoigwe's music will be discussed further under the subheading, thematic process. The idea of a tone row is not new to Uzoigwe considering his musical background in *ukom* music. *Ukom* ensemble has a fixed scale of ten tones. The pitches are organized into basic sets to create a musical form by permutation, repetition, variation and improvisation. Example 6e shows the twelve-tone row of *Oja*.

Example 6e. Twelve-Tone row of *Oja*

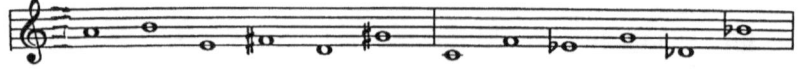

Like other Western composers of tonal music, Uzoigwe changes keys in his works. Most of his tonal works are characterized by this technique. He uses different tonal centers in his music to create various shades of sonorities and moods. For example, he uses only the keys of F# and G-flat (enharmonic of the former) majors for the ostinato sections in the *Nigerian Dances*. It may be that for him, this key is best for simulating melo/rhythmic sonorities of Igbo traditional musical instruments.[5] Uzoigwe also changes keys to delineate music sections. Hence, the change of tonal centers can serve as land marks for sectional analysis of his music. Below is a summary of *Nigerian Dances No. 2* showing the various tonal centers and how Uzoigwe begins in D minor and ends in C major.

Table 1. Tonal Centers in *Nigerian Dances No.2*

Measure	Key
1-6	D minor
7-11	A minor
12-14	D (tonal center)
15-31	C (tonal center)
32-45	D minor
46-65	C major
66-95	F# major (LH) F# minor (RH)
96-109	E (tonal Center)
116-125	B major
126-141	C major

---

[5] Melo/rhythm instruments are referred to as talking or language communication instruments such as the Igbo twin bells, wooden slit drum, membrane drums and the Yoruba talking drums (see Nzewi 1991:129).

Some of Uzoigwe's music involves a simultaneous combination of two keys. Works with bitonal sections include *A Sketch For Trombone* (measures 1-38), *Eriri Ngeringe* (measures 8-27), and *Nigerian Dances No. 2* (measures 66 to 95). In *A Sketch For Trombone*, the left hand of the piano accompaniment tonicizes B-flat major, while the right hand is in D major. The trombone part combines the two keys. The left hand of the *Nigerian Dances No. 2* is in F# major and the right hand in F# minor. The simultaneous combination of major and minor keys in a single work is also found in the music of Alban Berg (Wozzeck, opera in three acts), whose work Uzoigwe studied while at Guildhall (Machlis 1979:264). The vocal line of *Eriri Ngeringe* is in D minor, while the piano accompaniment is mostly in D major. Example 7 shows bitonality in *A Sketch For Trombone*. Notice bitonality especially in the piano accompaniment.

Example 7. Bitonality in *A Sketch For Trombone*
mm. 19-22

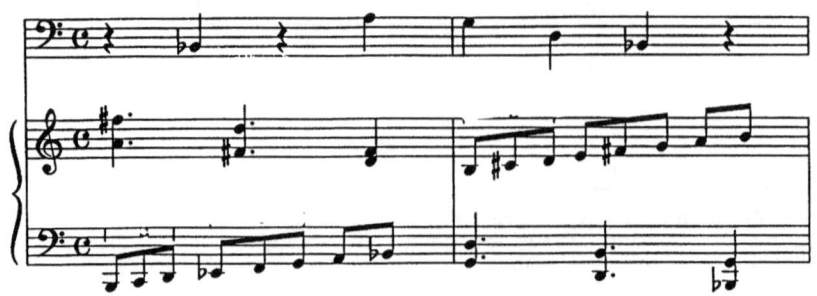

Vocal Range

The vocal range of most of Uzoigwe's songs is an octave, a compound second or a compound third. Songs within the range of an octave are most common. These include *Uyaroma, Ite Etipia Etipia,* and the bass solo in *Watermaid.* A wider interval such as ninth is found in the four vocal parts of the *Sirene Limits.* The *Four Igbo Songs* are based on Igbo folksongs which are generally within the range of an octave (Ekwueme 1980:105). The various vocal ranges in Uzoigwe's music are shown in examples 8a to 8c.

Example 8a. Vocal Range of *Uyaroma*

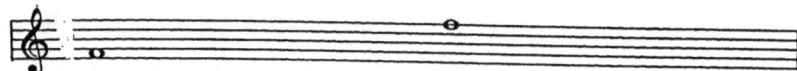

Example 8b. Vocal Range of *Watermaid*

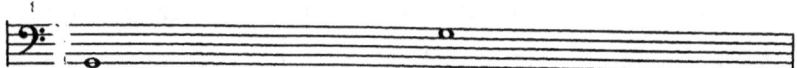

Example 8c. Vocal Ranges of *Sirene Limits* (Soprano and Tenor)

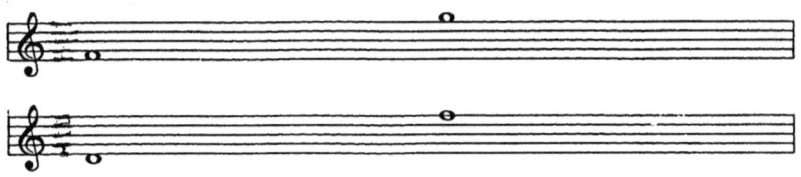

Harmonic Organization

Harmony in Uzoigwe's music is characterized by a variety of intervals such as 2nds and 7ths (secundal), 3rds and 6ths (tertian), 4ths and fifths (quartal) and tritones. The logical organization of these intervals constitutes Uzoigwe's harmonic vocabulary.

Secundal harmony

Second and seventh intervals in Uzoigwe's music appear in major and minor forms. He uses these chords to emphasize the percussive aspect of the musical instruments, especially the piano. Major or minor seconds and major sevenths are also used in evoking melo/rhythmic nuances of African traditional instruments. It is the clashing of the dissonance that effect percussiveness. Uzoigwe likewise employs percussive harmony to heighten tension in his music. The use of seconds has been noted in the singing style of the Ijesha-Yoruba of Nigeria and the Nguu of Tanzania (Nketia 1974:164). Uzoigwe often interlocks seconds with other types of chords such as fourths and thirds, to create a piquant sonority. The alternation of seconds with other consonant chords further avoids the monotony that could result from continuous dissonance (see example 9).

Example 9. Interlocking Seconds in *Eriri Ngeringe* (piano)
m. 3

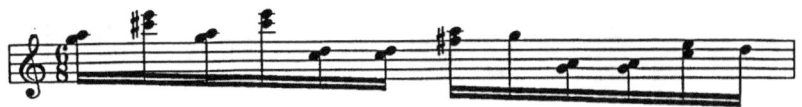

Seconds in Uzoigwe's music usually resolve down or up by half or whole step. The two notes may resolve at the same time with the top note moving up to the next note while the bottom one moves down to the next note. On the other hand, the two notes may resolve together on the same note. This kind of chord resolving is found in *Eriri Ngeringe, Ite Etipia Etipia* and in *Tuzu* (examples 10a to 10c show the two types of resolving seconds).

Example 10a. Resolving Seconds in *Ite Etipia Etipia*
m. 24

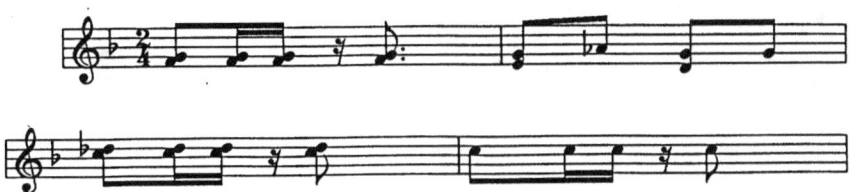

Example 10b. Resolving Seconds in *Eriri Ngeringe*
m. 21

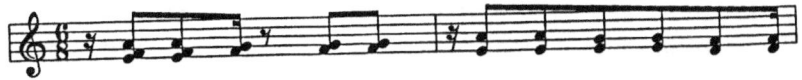

Example 10c. Resolving Seconds in *Tuzu*

m. 8

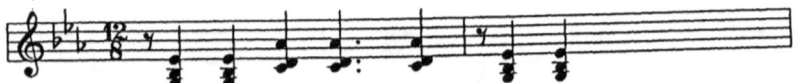

There are instances when seconds are not resolved, but are just left hanging. Unresolved seconds can be found in *Watermaid* (measures 2, 20-21 and 175-181), *Eriri Ngeringe* (measures 15 and 16), and *Sirene Limits* (measures 18-21 and 50-52). Example 11 below shows additional unresolved 2nds in *Watermaid.*

Example 11. Unresolved Seconds in *Watermaid*

mm. 2-3, 7-8

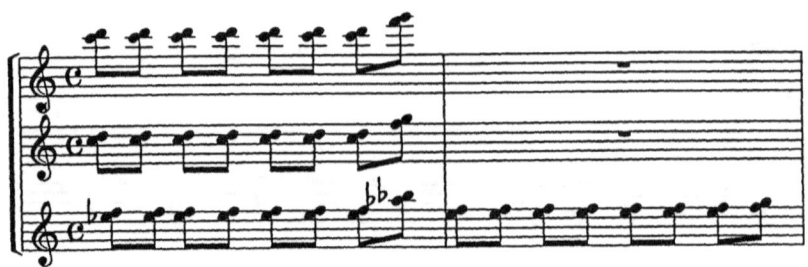

Tertian Harmony

Triadic harmony predominates Uzoigwe's tonal music. Works with this type of harmony include *Four Igbo Songs, Nigerian Dances For Piano, Sirene Limits*--all written between 1973 in Nigeria and 1976 in the United Kingdom. Chords of thirds are mostly in parallel form.

In Igbo music, there is a preponderance of chordal intervals of thirds as the primary traditional concord (Nzewi 1991:126). Tertian harmony sometime moves chromatically as in the soprano part of *Sirene Limits* (measures 31-32, and 39-40) and in the right hand of *Nigerian Dances No. 4* (measures 12 and 16). Example 12 shows chromatic motion of thirds in *Sirene Limits*.

Example 12. Chromatic motion of Thirds in *Sirene Limits*
m. 31

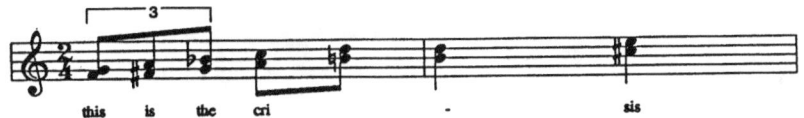

Chords of thirds move diatonically with or without another chord placed above it as in *Sirene Limits* (measures 46 and 47) and *Nigerian Dances No.3* (measures 10-11, and 14-15). Example 13 below depicts diatonic motion of thirds in *Sirene Limits*.

Example 13. Diatonic motion of Thirds in *Sirene Limits*
mm. 46, 47

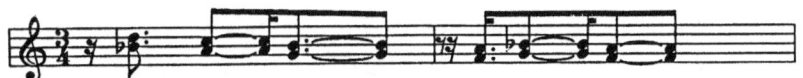

Static tertian chords are often supported by other chords before and after. In other words, they are approached and resolved by other harmonic forms--interlocking thirds. A good example of this is seen in *Nigerian Dances No.4* (measures 1 and 3). See example 14.

Example 14. Interlocking Thirds in *Nigerian Dances No.4*
mm. 1,3

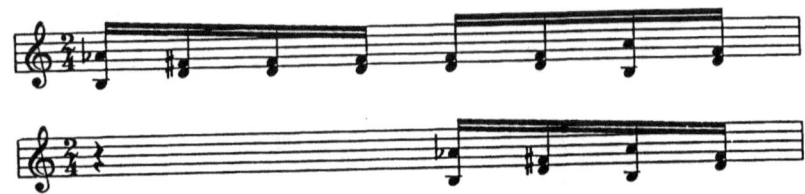

Quartal Harmony

Quartal harmony in Uzoigwe's music includes chords of fourths and fifths. Harmonic structures of fourths and fifths are some of the characteristic features of Igbo music (Ekwueme 1974:21). One obvious consequence of quartals is the simulation of the sonorous sound of the xylophone in Igbo tradition. These chords are either consonants or dissonants. Consonant quartals appear as perfect fourths and perfect fifths while dissonant quartals appear as tritones and augmented fifths. There is evidence of quartal harmony in the *Sirene Limits, Ite Etipia Etipia, Tuzu, Grand Little One,Watermaid* and the *Nigerian Dances.*

Quartals in the music of Uzoigwe often move in strict parallel motion. Uzoigwe's usage is similar in style to the strict organum of Western music of the eleventh and twelfth centuries with the second voice or instrumental part imitating the rise and fall of the melodic part strictly. However, in the Nigerian context, it is the inflectionary character of the speech patterns that necessitates parallelism. If the second voice part is to maintain the meaning of the words of a song, then it must imitate the melodic leaps of the first voice part strictly. Any deviation from this pattern would result in the soloist and his accompaniment singing two different things (Akpabot 1986:104). What Uzoigwe has done is the epitomization of this vocal technique in his works. He uses the concept of parallelism in both vocal and instrumental works. Examples 15a and 15b are representative of parallelism in Uzoigwe's instrumental music.

Example 15a. Parallel Motion of Quartal Harmony in *Watermaid*
m. 145

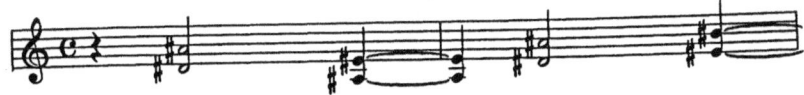

m. 206

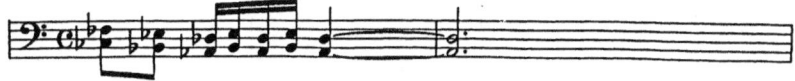

Example 15b. Parallel Motion of Quartals in *Grand Little One*
m. 14

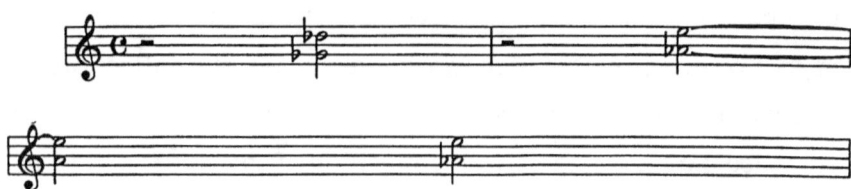

Another harmonic device in Uzoigwe's music is the use of three note chords consisting of fourths and fifths. Three intervallic arrangements of fourths and fifths are possible: perfect-perfect, perfect-augmented, and augmented-perfect. Uzoigwe features only the first type--perfect-perfect--in his music. Notice perfect fourths over perfect fifths in example 16.

Example 16. Fourth and Fifth Chords in *Watermaid*
m. 103

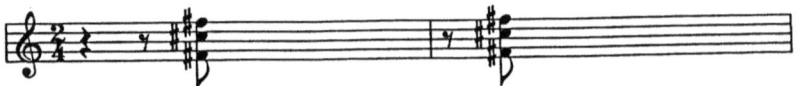

Thematic Process

One of the most interesting features of Uzoigwe's music is the process through which he establishes and develops thematic materials. The root of this technique is embedded in Western and African compositional procedures. An overview of Uzoigwe's music reveals the trait of motivic development of prime cells. Generally, he introduces the basic set/s at the beginning of the piece and then proceeds to use various devices to expand and vary them. Some of the developmental techniques adopted by Uzoigwe in his music are permutation of basic sets, thematic variation, imitation, and transposition. Other forms of developmental processes include inversion, retrograde and retrograde inversion. Nzewi, for example, has shown that,

> The driving energy and the physical intensity of most Igbo music are primarily contained and sustained by a principle of thematic development based on internal variations (Nzewi 1991:109).

Euba goes on to argue that the most important single element characteristic of extended forms of composition designed for contemplation is the element of variation (Euba 1992:316). The idea of thematic development in Uzoigwe's music can be regarded as a translation of traditional procedures into a new socio-musical context. In other words, the process through which he develops his musical ideations is experiential and cultural. Igbo musical composition is a situational variable because the performers, although using substructural constants, are creative variables (Nzewi 1991:108). This device is atypical of Western classical tradition where a composition and its performers are both defined constant. Igbo music is therefore, judged not by its quality as an interpretative reproduction of a fixed or finished composition, rather by its interest as a fresh composition, that is, as a contextual re-composition of a model compositional framework. The various developmental procedures stated above can be seen in most compositions by Uzoigwe. Thus, rather than taking examples in bits and pieces from different works, I intend to show how Uzoigwe deploys the technique in two works, *Sketches For Piano No. 2* and *Ritual Procession.*

Thematic Process In *Sketches For Piano No. 2.*

Sketches For Piano No. 2 is one of the pieces written by Uzoigwe when at the Guildhall School of Music, London. It is based on a predetermined twelve tone row. The piece is based on three melo/rhythmic motifs which appear in the first three measures. See example 17 for the three motifs. The rest of the music is based on reshufflings and permutations of the basic sets.

Example 17. Three Motifs of *Sketches For Piano No.2*
m. 1,2

A   B

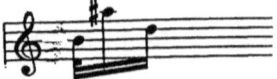
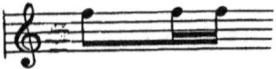

m. 3

C

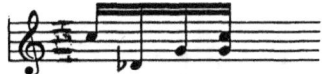

We can see the transposed versions of motif A in measures 6 and 7. In the two instances the motif is transposed up a minor third, and down an augmented fourth respectively (See example 18).

Example 18. Transposed Version of Motif A

m. 6

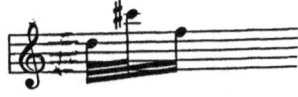

As examples 19a and 19b show, there is an evidence of intervallic reduction of the last two pitches in measures 8 and 15, while there is intervallic expansion of the first two pitches in measures 12 and 13.

Example 19a. Intervallic Reduction of Motif A

m. 8   m. 15

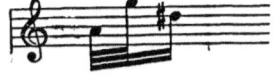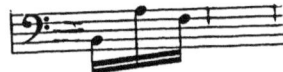

Example 19b. Intervallic Expansion of Motif A

m. 12   m. 13

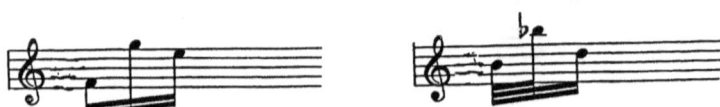

Varied versions of motif B are in measures 7 and 18 at different pitch levels, with augmented fourth and diminished fifth harmonization (see example 20a).

Example 20a. Varied Versions of Motif B

mm. 7,18

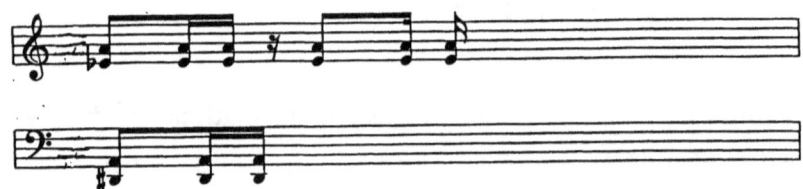

Motif B is monophonic without harmonic accompaniment in measures 9 and 10, while measure 15 is an exact repetition of measure 7 (see example 20b).

Example 20b. Motif B in Unison

m. 10

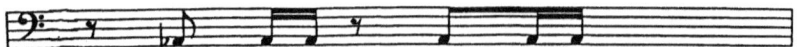

Motif C is repeated exactly in its primary form throughout the whole piece. It is merely traded between the left and right hands at the same pitch level and with the same notes (see example 21).

Example 21. Motif C

m. 12

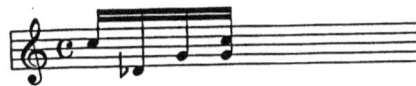

Ritual Procession

The *Ritual Procession* is a type of aleatoric music. Similar to *Sketches For Piano No. 2,* it is based on melo/rhythmic cells established at the beginning of the music. The piece which Uzoigwe constructs on fifty-two melo/rhythmic cells is meant to be performed by as many instrumentalists in a quasi-canonic style. Each pattern of the cells is derived from a well-known rhythmic pattern called the West African time-line (or the konkonkonlo rhythm among the Yoruba). Traditionally, this rhythmic pattern is assigned to a double bell. The bells repeat the pattern constantly throughout the entire duration of the performance (see example 22 for the basic rhythmic cell).

Example 22. Basic Rhythmic Pattern of *Ritual Procession*

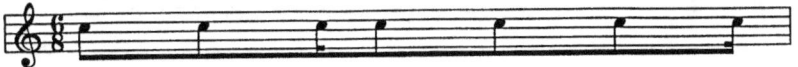

Each player dwells on each variant pattern as long as he chooses, progressing from one pattern to another in the order presented in the score and taking his bearing from the main pulse established by the bell. The result of these activities is an interplay of rhythmic patterns, textures and waves of dissonant harmonies, giving one the aural impression of a fusion of sounds from different instruments in a festive procession--hence the title. The free form suggests derivation of perpetual variation technique called *ilulu nkwa* (musical proverb) in *ukom* music of the Igbo. The dynamic contrasts between instruments result mainly from the pitching of the tonal strength of one instrument against the other. Example 23 shows the variants derived from the basic cell.

Example 23a. Variants of the Basic Pattern with Different Pitches
Pattern 18

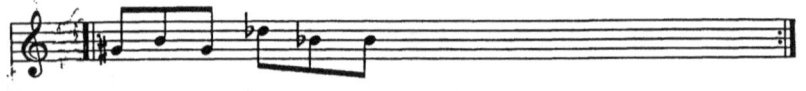

Pattern 26

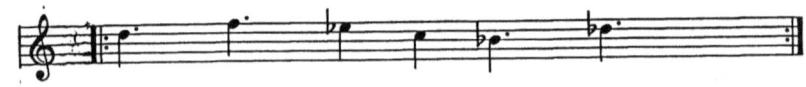

Pattern 28

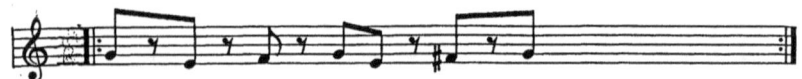

Pattern 46

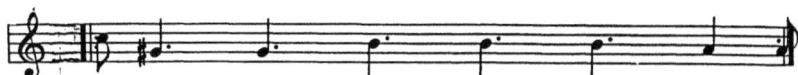

Example 23b. Prime Cell Derived from Basic Pattern and its Variants

Pattern 1

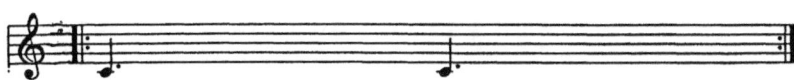

Pattern 5

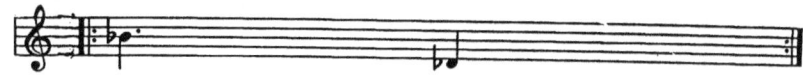

Pattern 10

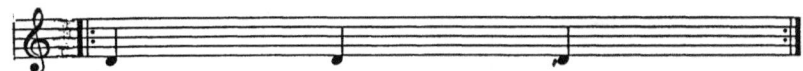

Pattern 11

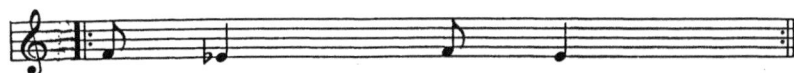

Example 23c. Variants of Prime Cell Derived from Basic Pattern

Pattern 4

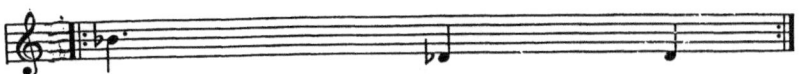

Pattern 7

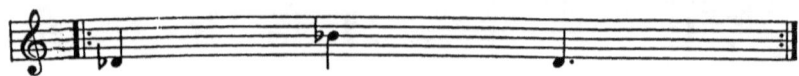

Pattern 42

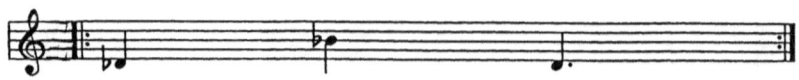

Pattern 6

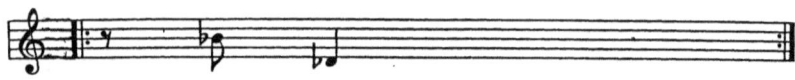

Some of the techniques adopted by Uzoigwe in processing the motifs in the *Ritual Procession* are augmentation of note values (pattern 26), variation through the use of interlocking rests and dotted notes (patterns 28 and 46), additive and divisive rhythmic variation (patterns 10 and 11), and retrogade technique (pattern 7).

Another type of thematic usage in Uzoigwe's music is the employment of folk tunes as principal theme. Prominent among these works are the *Nigerian Dances Nos. 2* and *3*. The principal theme in *Nigerian Dances No.2* is a derivation of a Yoruba church anthem called *Ise Oluwa* (composed by Dr. Thomas Ekundayo Philips, one of the pioneering church organists in Nigeria).

The principal theme in *Nigerian Dances No. 3* is taken from a Yoruba folktune known as *Olurounbi*.

The issue of cultural identity and the search for an African audience are some of the problems Uzoigwe attempts to solve in his compositions. Nigerian folk tunes are employed to provide cultural base for the works and to bring the compositions closer to the African traditional roots. Alan Lomax (1976:9) notes that the salient features of song are symbols for the key institutions of society. Folksongs, therefore, in modern works such as African art music, identify and reinforce core structure of society.

The use of folk tunes in Uzoigwe's music is an extension of the efforts by pioneering African church organists and choirmasters. As we may recall in chapter two, early church organists employ indigenous African musical elements to relate the congregation to the music. The experiment was and is still in line with the spirit of nationalism which pervaded Africa in the early sixties. In other words, the use of traditional musical elements such as folk tunes is one of the ways modern African composers use in avoiding total Western hegemony in their work.

Nketia (1982:83) and Omojola (1995:166) observe that modern compositions which are infused with rhythmic, melodic and formal elements of African music will elicit a positive response from an African audience. Such a response can be derived from the appreciation of the musical structure of the works as well as their relevance to any extra-musical ideas or contexts (religious or secular) and any emotional reactions associated with such contexts. The issue of audience relation to Uzoigwe's music is further discussed in chapter 5.

Finally, the employment of folk tunes attracts African performers (both singers and instrumentalists) to the works. The well known tune in the pieces enables the singer or pianist to learn the music faster. The presence of the folk tune gives a sense of simplicity because the performers are familiar with the rhythmic disposition, structure and melodic phrases in the work. From experience, the author finds it easy to learn African piano pieces with indigenous folk tunes as main theme than abstract ones--pieces not based on popular folk tunes. See examples 1a, 1b, 4a and 4b for excerpts of Nigerian folksongs.

Cadences

Three basic cadential devices are observed in Uzoigwe's music. These are conventional Western cadences such as perfect authentic and semi cadences. The third type is avoidance of cadential points. The first two cadences are observed in the *Sirene Limits, Nigerian Dances* and *Four Igbo Songs.* The cadences are generally chord progressions of dominant/dominant seventh to tonic and tonic to dominant. Examples 24a to 24d show the two types of cadences. The dominant chord in Example 24a deviates slightly from the traditional formula because of the tonic F. The dominant C chord passes through A-flat before resolving on F.

Example 24a Perfect Authentic Cadence in *Uyaroma*
m. 5

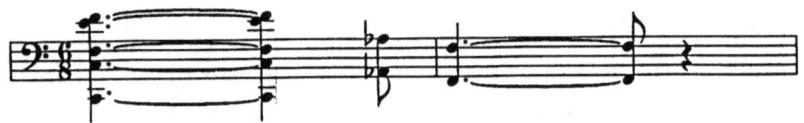

Example 24b Perfect Authentic Cadence in *Nigerian Dances No.3*
m. 15

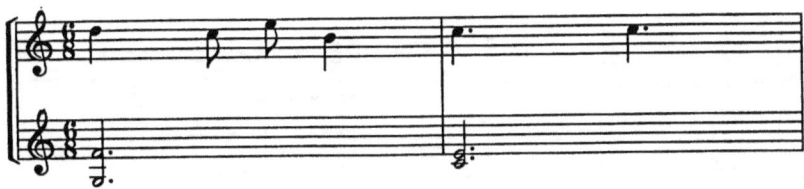

Example 24c Semi Cadence in *Eriri Ngeringe*
m. 44

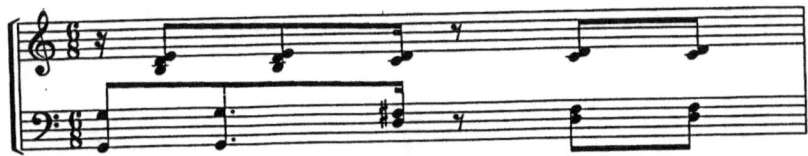

The technique of avoiding cadential points is prominently featured in all works by Uzoigwe. Taking the *Nigerian Dances No.2* for illustration, he uses octave progressions, chromatic motions, ostinato patterns, and rests at cadential points to displace functional harmony. Measures 12 to 14 reveal how Uzoigwe simultaneously uses octave and chromatic motion to avoid resolving at point of cadence (see examples 25a and 25b). This trait is likewise seen in chromatic motion between measures 46 to 49 and measures 62 to 65. In example 25b, rather than resolving on the dominant chord in measure 47, the melody is accompanied with a chromatic motion in the left hand to avoid a semi cadence.

Example 25a Avoiding of Cadential point in *Nigerian Dances No.2* m. 12-14

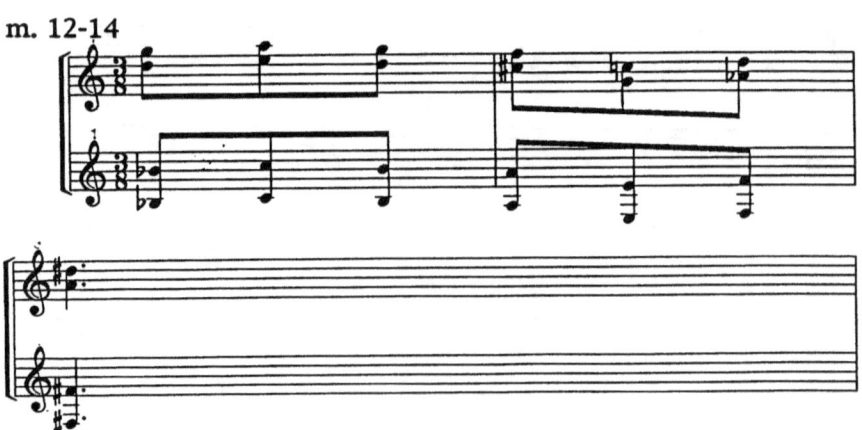

Example 25b Avoiding of Cadential Point in *Nigerian Dances No.2* m. 46-47

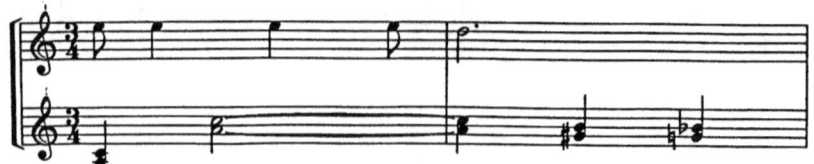

Measures 72 to 95 in *Nigerian Dances No.2* show how Uzoigwe uses ostinato to displace functional harmony. The persistently repeated melo/rhythmic pattern in the bass does not permit harmonic consonance at appropriate cadential points. Consequently, melodic pitches could not resolve at cadential positions. The ostinato firmly anchors the melodic motion with the repeats and low F sharps acting as a drone (see example 26).

Example 26 Avoiding of Cadential Point in *Nigerian Dances No.2* mm. 72-77

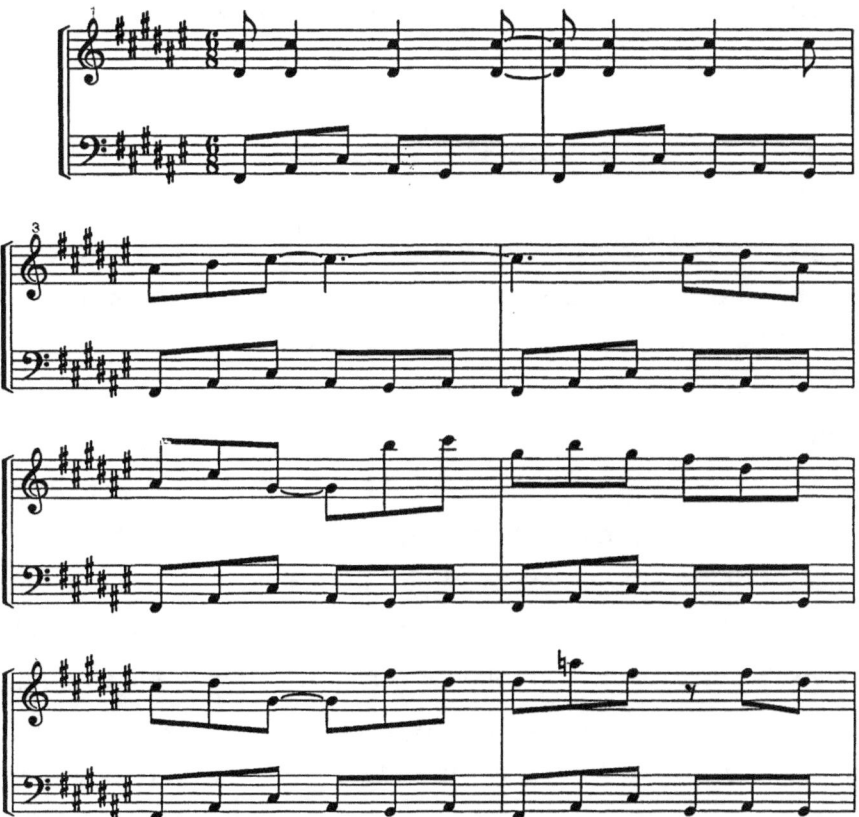

The avoidance of cadences is likewise observed in the music of Richard Wagner and some twentieth century Western composers. Uzoigwe's creative impulse is influenced both by these composers and by Nigerian traditional music, in which cadential points found in eighteenth-and-nineteenth century European music are irrelevant. Local musicians have special methods of closing music at given points which differ from that of Western music. The reason for this is that at the point of musical conception, traditional musicians do not conceive the tonal organization of their music in terms of functional harmony (chords I, IV and V). They employ distinctive rhythmic patterns and gesticulations to close music at specific points.

Rhythmic Organization

Uzoigwe uses different types of rhythmic structures to shape his music. Among these are polyrhythms, syncopated rhythms, and interlocking rhythms.

Polyrhythms

Most of Uzoigwe's music is characterized by polyrhythms. He combines different types of rhythmic patterns in each work to give it life and vitality. One of the most interesting polyrhythmic usages in Uzoigwe's music is the interplay of constant and variable rhythms. What makes repetition exciting in his music is the simultaneous interaction of rhythmic variations and repetitions over a time span.

Often, Uzoigwe assigns repetitive rhythmic patterns to accompaniment, like an ostinato, and variations to melodic line. This technique is observed in *Nigerian Dances Nos. 1, 2* and *4*. The *Four Igbo Songs* in the same manner, features a type of quasi-ostinato best shown in the cyclic shape of the piano accompaniments with varied rhythmic patterns of the songs (melodic lines). Examples 27a and 27b show the constant (ostinato) in the bass and the varied (melody) in the treble of *Nigerian Dances Nos. 1* and *2*.

Example 27a Variable and Constant Rhythms in *Nigerian Dances No.1* m. 15

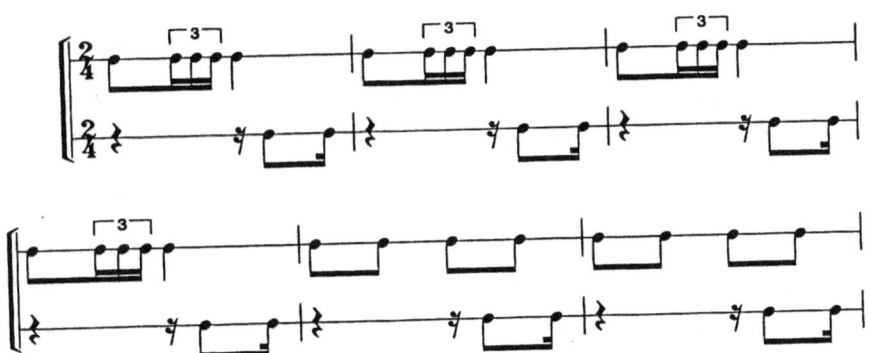

Example 27b Variable and Constant Rhythms in *Nigerian Dances No.2*
m. 72

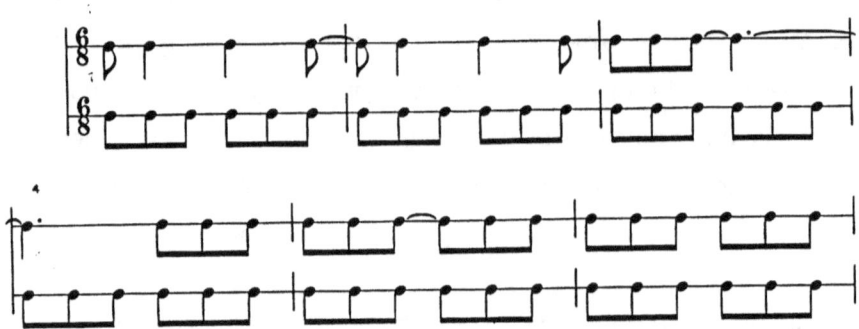

A closer look at *Nigerian Dances No.1* shows that the constant is not
repeated exactly the same way throughout the piece. In other
words, there is an element of variation within the constant line. In
example 27a, the first rhythmic pattern in the bass (♪♪♪♪) is
omitted, leaving the second part intact (𝄾 ♪ ♪ ♪). The resting
point in the bass is filled in the treble line, creating a kind of call-and
-response between the two lines. The technique of omission within a
time space is commonly found in African traditional musical
processes. This technique is similar to William Anku's concept of
waiting patterns. Anku describes a waiting pattern as an abstraction
from a main pattern serving in some ways as a resting point for the
performer. It is used to 'suffix' or to extend a sequence of patterns
constituting a coherent rhythmic statement (Anku 1995:175).

The role of ostinato passages in Uzoigwe's music is similar to the role played by secondary drums in an African ensemble. For instance, the second set of drums/tones in *ukom* music (that is, 6 to 10) functions primarily as a means of composing melodic variations and projecting the principal themes of the songs. The other five drums (1 to 5) supply the cyclic accompaniment--ostinato (Uzoigwe 1986:55). Constant and variable technique in Uzoigwe's music is reminiscent of xylophone music of the Chopi, where each of the three or four supporting sets of xylophones plays an ostinato pattern in support of the main melody, while the leader plays improvised variations (Nketia 1974:123).

Syncopations

Uzoigwe uses syncopated rhythms in his music to create motion for dance. Syncopation distorts regular beat pulsations but gives direction to the music. The effect of syncopations will be discussed further under the subheading, interrelations of music and dance. Examples of syncopated rhythms in Uzoigwe's music are as follows (examples 28a and 28b):

Example 28a Syncopations in *A Sketch For Trombone*
mm. 7-9

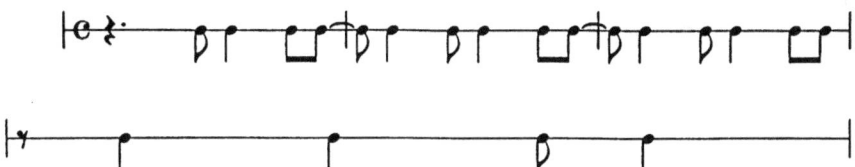

Example 28b Syncopations in *Watermaid* (oboe)
mm. 234-238

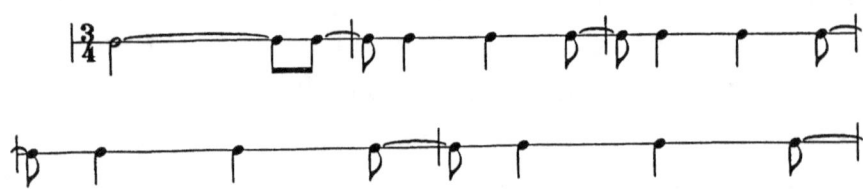

Interlocking Rhythms

Uzoigwe employs interlocking rhythmic structures like the
syncopated rhythms, to create motion for dance and suggest a
participatory audience experience. The interlocked rhythms may be
on one or two lines. For instance, the rhythms are placed only in the
treble line of *Sketches For Piano No.1* and between the left and right
hand in the piano accompaniment of *Tuzu,* one of the *Four Igbo
Songs.* Interlocking rhythms can also be seen in *Sketches For Piano
No. 4.* Examples 29a and 29b show interlocking rhythms in
Uzoigwe's music.

Example 29a Interlocking Rhythms in *Tuzu*
mm. 8-9

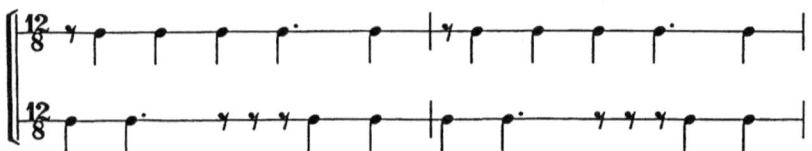

Example 29b Interlocking Rhythms in *Sketches For Piano No.4*
mm. 12-13

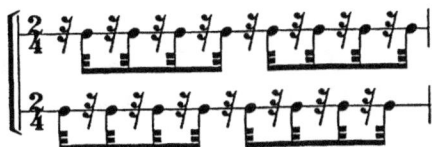

Texture

We distinguished three types of texture in Uzoigwe's music, namely, monophonic, homophonic and polyphonic textures. The three types of textures are never to be found indepedently, rather, they are mostly used alternately in his music. The compass of Uzoigwe's music is likewise considered in this section.

Monophony

Most of Uzoigwe's works are homophonic and polyphonic in texture, however, we can see some phrases or measures of monophony within a work. Monophony in Uzoigwe's music is similar to the music of India and the Arab world, China and Japan, Java and Bali, whose music up to a thousand years ago was monophonic (Machlis 1979:35). Single-voice texture is also similar to the monophonic period of Western music, that is, the fifteen-hundred-year-old liturgical music of the Catholic Church, the Gregorian chant. Monophonic texture (in which octave doublings may be considered) is observed in *Sketches For Piano Nos. 1* and *3, Watermaid, Sketches*

For *Trombone,* and some of the *Nigerian Dances. Sketches For Piano Nos. 1* and *3* are conceived mostly in monophonic style. See examples 30a and 30b for monophony in Uzoigwe's music.

Example 30a Monophony in *Sketches For Piano No.3*
mm. 5-7

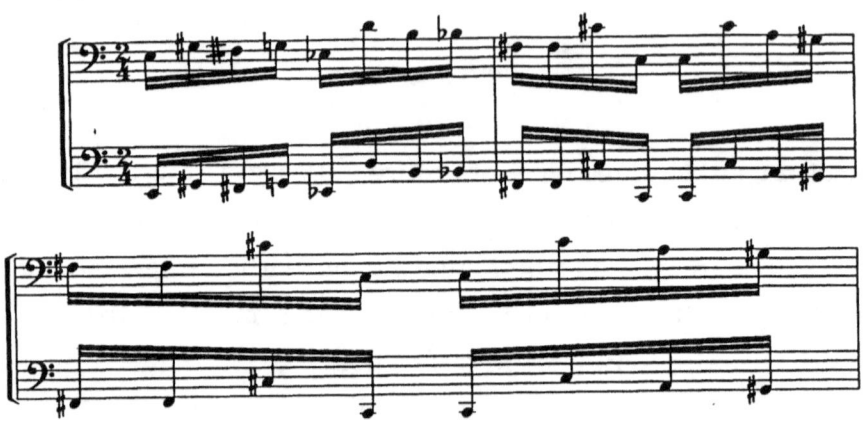

Example 30b Monophony in *Watermaid* (Cello and Bass)
mm. 5-8

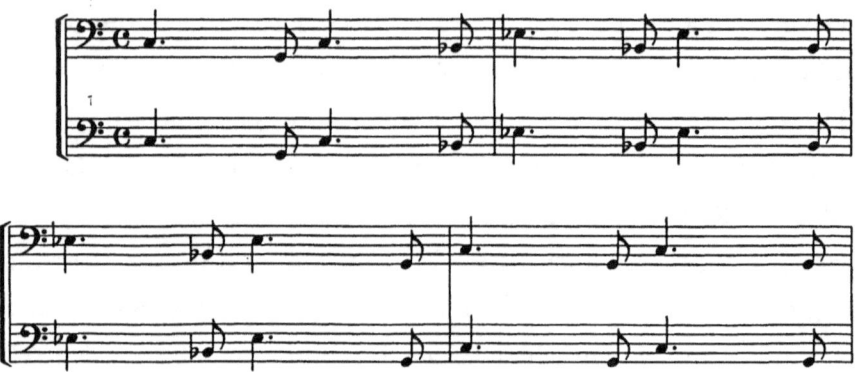

Homophony

Apart from works such as *Oja* and *Sketches For Piano,* most of
Uzoigwe's music is homophonic in texture. The vocal and
instrumental pieces follow the style of song and accompaniment.
There is a constant interplay of independent melodic line with
harmonic or melo/rhythmic accompaniment. It is easy for the
listeners to perceive the single line of melody in Uzoigwe's music.
The melody is not always conceived as a self-sufficient entity, but
with continuous dependence on the supporting vertical harmony or
melo/rhythms from the accompaniment. Melody is consistently
emphasized and often set apart from the rest of the texture (See
examples 31a to 31c).

Example 31a Homophony in *Nigerian Dances No.3*
mm. 1-4

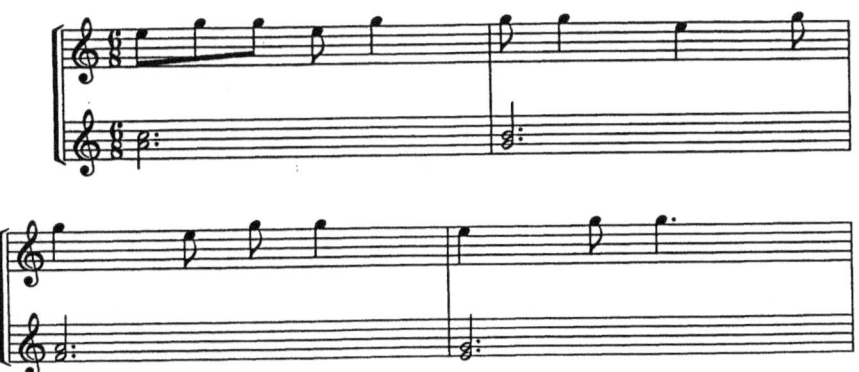

Example 31b Homophony in *A Sketch For Trombone*
mm. 3-5

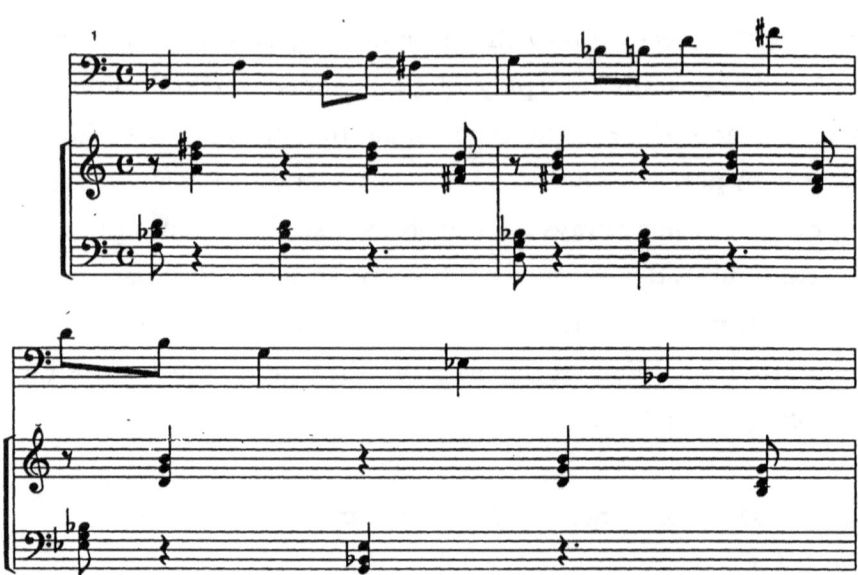

Example 31c Homophony in *Grand Little One* (SATB)
mm. 2-4

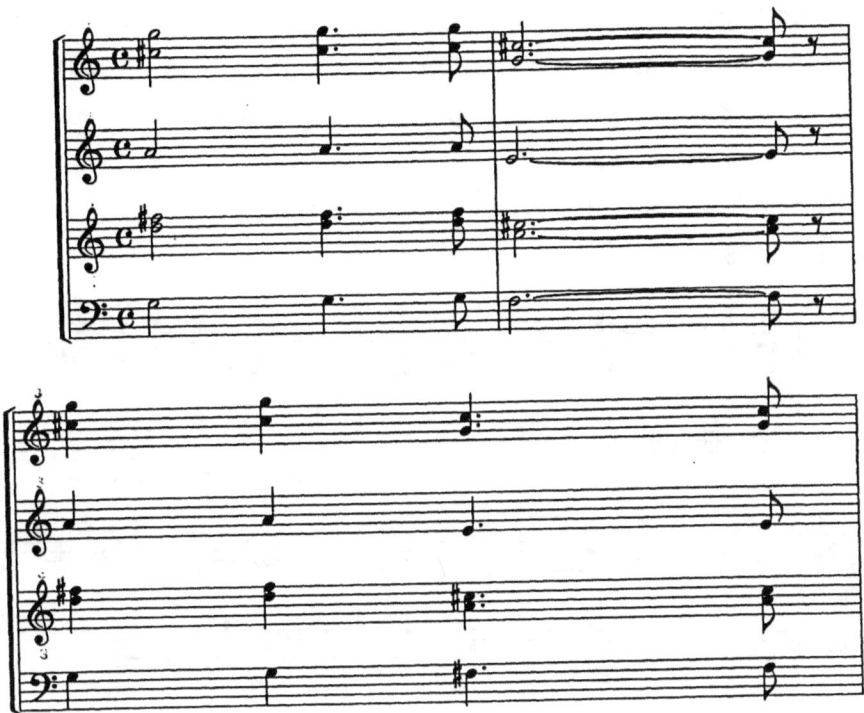

Polyphony

Polyphonic texture in Uzoigwe's music is intertwined with homophonic texture. Though his music is homophonic generally, the independence of each line lends itself to contrapuntal style. Rhythmically, each line is independent of one another. Uzoigwe cleverly combines several melodic lines in a unified musical fabric.

The beauty of contrapuntal style in his music is the contrasting rhythmic structures of independent voices. Polyphony in Uzoigwe's music is similar to the Lobi xylophone music in which the right hand generally plays the main melody while the left hand accompanies it with a figure based on a counter-rhythm (Nketia 1974:123). See examples 32a and 32b for polyphony in Uzoigwe's music.

Example 32a Polyphony in *Nigerian Dances No.4*
mm. 62-65

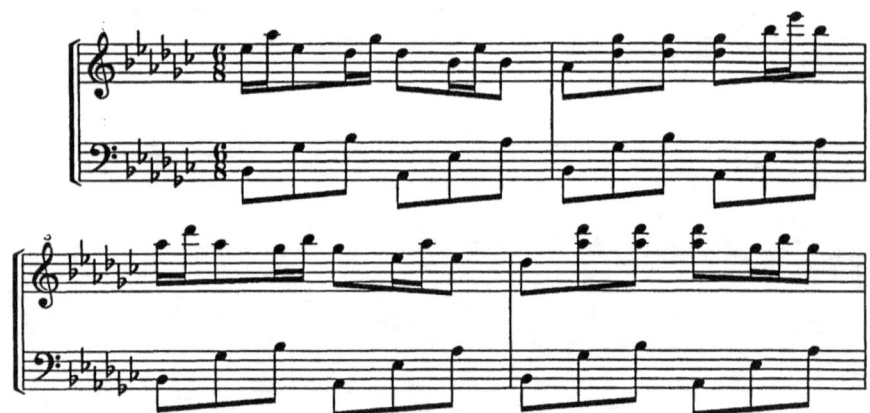

Example 32b Polyphony in *Sketches For Piano No.3*
mm. 9-11

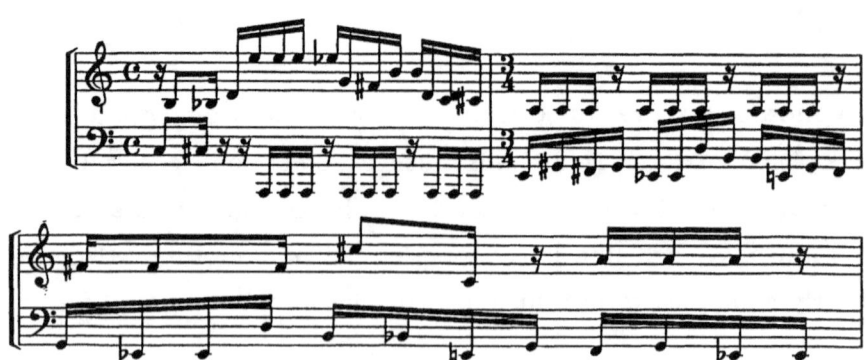

Compass

The range of Uzoigwe's music generally is between four and five octaves. Both the vocal and instrumental pieces are within this compass. From observation, most of his vocal works are within medium range (three to four octaves[6]), while the instrumental ones have the wider range (four to five octaves). In addition, Uzoigwe's music tends to begin in either a middle register or high register and closes mostly in the low and high registers etc... The vocal pieces often begin from middle or high registers and ends on middle or high registers. The instrumental works usually begin from a low or high point and close most often on high or low point. In between the opening and closing end of the works, the music usually spreads out to higher, lower or middle registers. In other words, a work might begin at a low register, moves to a high point and then contract to a middle register. This zig zag motion may continue like this before the piece finally finds repose at its destination. The graphical illustration in figure 1 shows expansions and contractions of registers in *Nigerian Dances No.2* (measures 1 to 18). The top line represents the right hand, while the lower line represents the left hand. The two hands start on the same note D with the left hand an octave apart from the right. The right hand ends on C above the middle C, while the left hand ends on A-flat below middle C.

---

[6] I mean the range in choral music when all parts are taken into account.

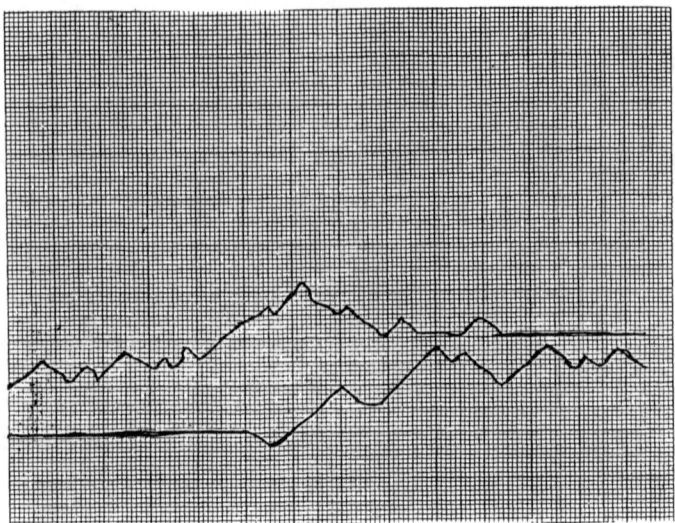

Figure 1. Pitch waves in *Nigerian Dances No.2*

Form

Form in the music of Uzoigwe adheres slightly to conventions of Western music and more to the formal structure of traditional music in Africa. Critical observation shows that he adopts mainly Western ternary form, and African through-composed and free-form techniques.

Most of Uzoigwe's vocal works (*Four Igbo Songs, Watermaid,Sirene Limits,* and *Grand Little One*) are through-composed or in ternary form, whereas, the instrumental are mostly in free-form.

We were dealing with form in discussing factors such as rhythmic organization, constant and variable in his music.

The shape of Uzoigwe's music is both determined by conventional structures and his personality.

Structurally speaking, most of Uzoigwe's music is in free-form. Free-form in Uzoigwe's music can be divided into works which are through-composed and works with sectional constant and variable phrases. It is a type of quasi-rondo. By through-composed I mean works with no distinct sectional repetition. As regards free-form, Uzoigwe explains that it is

> form in movement, charged with emotive impetus that is reminiscent of African traditional performance-composition and seem to run the whole gamut of human feelings (Uzoigwe 1992:57).

The sort of variation described by Uzoigwe here is similar to the concept of perpetual variation, meaning the principle of continuous mutation and elaboration of a given quantity of material. Uzoigwe adopts free-form in most of his music because form is not conceptualized by the traditional Igbo musician as being a pre-established framework which is set out to determine the shape of the music. Rather, it is the resultant shape created by the musicians' moulding of their musical conceptions in conformity to the social event structure with which the music and/or musical performance is associated (Uzoigwe 1988:65). Consequently, form in Igbo music is conceptualized more as a process than as a static product. *Nigerian*

Dances No.3 is a good specimen for works with sectional constants and variables. Figure 2 shows sectional divisions of the piece.

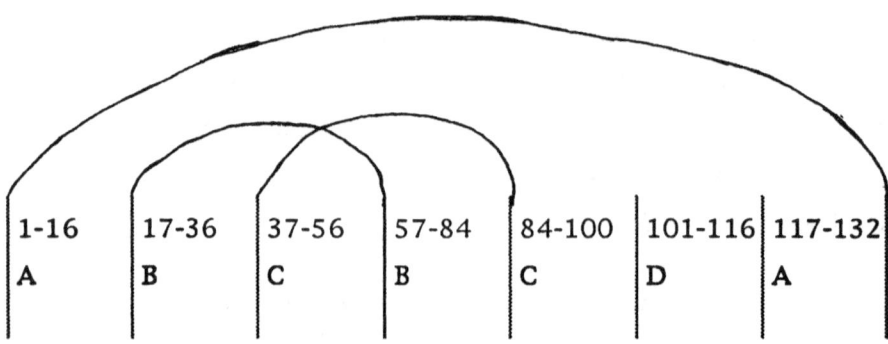

1-16	17-36	37-56	57-84	84-100	101-116	117-132
A	B	C	B	C	D	A

Figure 2. Free-form of *Nigerian Dances No.3*

Table 2. Sectional division in *Nigerian Dances No.3*

Sections	Description
A	Principal theme (Yoruba folksong-*Olurounbi*)
B	Variant of principal theme with dissonances
C	New theme
B	Restatement of B
C	Restatement of C
D	Another new theme
A	Recapitulation of principal theme

The use of contrasting sections in *Nigerian Dances No.3* is similar to the idea of creating a new song or tune within the framework of an on-going piece of music in African tradition. It is reminiscent of African traditional performance-composition in which the master musician in the context of musical performance can shift from one song to another, but may finally return to the original tune or song at the end. For instance, *ukom* music of the Igbo consists of three distinct sections, *ilulu nkwa, ogbe nkwa* and *ihu nkwa. Ogbe nkwa* and *ihu nkwa* sections consist of several songs with each lasting for about ten seconds to one minute in duration. Often, the master musician will introduce *nkwa ika* (ancient music) and *abigbo* (current music or 'Igbo wit') into the music to extend the composition (Uzoigwe 1980:18,19).

Tempo And Meter

Tempo

Tempo in Uzoigwe's music can be classified into two main types, constant tempo and variable tempo. The former refers to works in which the tempo remains stable from beginning to the end, while variable tempo belongs to works with two or more fluctuating speeds within a music. In other words, variable tempo will have more than one tempo mark in a single work. Uzoigwe makes more use of constant tempos than variable tempos. Constant tempos are more prominent in his vocal works than the instrumental ones.

Works with constant tempos include *Four Igbo Songs, Watermaid* and *Oja,* while those with variable tempos are the *Nigerian Dances, Sketches For Piano,* and *A Sketch For Trombone.*

The frequently used tempo marks in Uzoigwe's music are moderato, allegretto and ritenuto. Uzoigwe adopts variable tempos in his music for three reasons: (1) to mark the end of a phrase or a section in the music, (2) to create drama through the use of tempo marks such as rubato, morendo and accelerando, finally (3) to add freshness to the music by dispensing with the monopoly of a dominant tempo.

Meter

As in the case of tempo in Uzoigwe's music, meter can likewise be divided into two main types, namely constant and variable meters. Contrary to what we found in his use of tempo, Uzoigwe's music is characterized by variable meter. The idea of changing meters might be an influence of Western composers on Uzoigwe. As we may recall from chapter three that he studied the works of twentieth century European composers while at Guildhall. Although, variable meter is found in most of his music, it is mostly associated with the instrumental works. The exertion of variable meter in Uzoigwe's music gives room for an interplay of diverse rhythmic patterns similar to African polyrhythms.

Metric systems in Uzoigwe's music are duple, triple, quadruple, and compound meters. Uzoigwe is fond of combining two or three of these meters in each of his works. It should not be surprising to find these meters in Uzoigwe's music since African rhythms generally have triple meters in the time of duple such as 12/8 (4/4) or 6/8 (2/4) (Akpabot 1986:84). A summary of variable meter in two works by Uzoigwe is shown in Tables 3 and 4.

Table 3. Variable Meter in *Nigerian Dances No.2*

Meter	Measure
3/8	1-45
3/4	46-71
6/8	72-141

Table 4. Variable Meter in *Sirene Limits*

Meter	Measure
2/4	20, 26-32, 34-36, 49-51
3/4	6-9
4/4	1-5, 10-19, 21-25, 33, 37-44, 48
6/8	45-47

Dynamics

The importance of dynamics is very crucial to the overall fabric of musical composition. A successful delivery, interpretation and perception of a work by its performers depends greatly on the placement of appropriate dynamics at proper positions. Composers, like Uzoigwe, often use dynamics to give direction and create drama in the music. Dynamic fluctuations are dictated by harmonic, melodic, and rhythmic progressions.

It is not surprising to experience consistent dynamic changes in works such as *Ite Etipia Etipia, Eriri Ngeringe, Sketches For Piano, Nigerian Dances* and *Watermaid* because of the frequent register shifts. In these works, Uzoigwe exploits the three main registral levels--low, middle and high respectively. Consequently, melodic motions revolving around these registers invariably demand appropriate dynamics that will best reflect the progressions. As illustration, Uzoigwe uses signs such as mp, p, pp, mf, and diminuendo to support melodic and harmonic line within the low and middle registers. Dynamics such as f, ff, sf and crescendo are mostly associated with pitches at high registers. See Table 5 as an illustration of dynamic fluctuations in Uzoigwe's music.

Table 5. Dynamic fluctuations in *Sirene Limits*

Dynamics	Measure	Register
mp	1-5	Middle-low
mf	6-7	Middle
p	8-9	Low-high on the word Silent fall
mp	10-19	Middle-Low
Cresc - Dim	19-21	Low
pp (ST) mp (AB)	22-30	(AB) Sings text, (ST) holds note-pedal
f	30-38	Low-high
mp-p	39-45	Low-high
mf-p	46-52	Middle-high

Uzoigwe uses only one dynamic sign in works where the melodic line seems to be even with little or no shift to different registers. Examples of such works are *Tuzu* and *Uyaroma*. The melodic lines of these pieces revolve around the middle register throughout the entire piece with hardly any visible shift to neighboring registers.

Textual meaning also dictates choice of dynamics in Uzoigwe's music. In the *Sirene Limits*, between measures 8 and 9, the melodic motion moves from a low point to a high point, but with p as the dynamic sign. He uses p to give meaning to the words 'silent, silent fall.' Obviuosly, one cannot use a fortissimo in this context to interpret the word 'silent,' it may sound awkward (See example 33).

Example 33. Text and Dynamics in *Sirene Limits*
m. 8

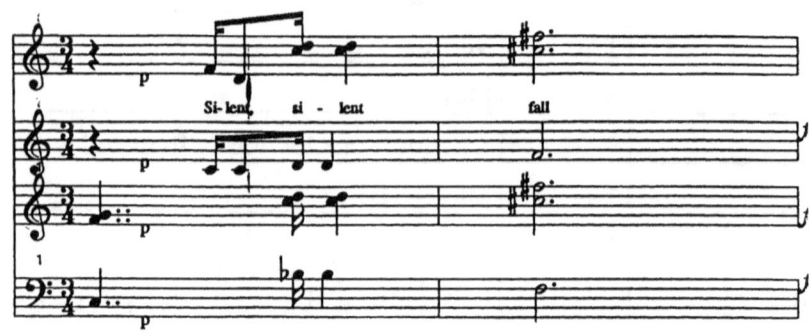

Still on the relations of text and dynamics, Uzoigwe gives different dynamics to individual voices in his vocal works to emphasize a certain text over the other. For example, in the *Sirene Limits*, Uzoigwe gives mp to alto and bass parts singing the text, while pp is assigned to soprano and tenor parts supplying harmonic background in the form of pedals to the former. This is done so that the text would be heard and not overshadowed by the supporting harmony. Dynamics reinforce the natural rhythm of melodic and harmonic lines. Using them at appropriate points create drama and sonorous sounds to listeners of the music.

Interrelations of Music And Dance

Scholars such as Nketia (1974), Akpabot (1986), Uzoigwe (1988), and
Nzewi (1991), have often stressed the indisputable relationships
between music and dance in Africa. Music that is associated with
bodily movements and responses are more common since Africans
belong to movement and speech communities. For the African, the
musical experience is by and large an emotional one. The aesthetics
of a good musical performance hinges on the motoristic response it
creates in the people. However, we do not shy away from the
recognition of contemplative music not designed for drama or dance.

In light of the preceeding argument, it should not be surprising to
note that most of Uzoigwe's music exhibit traits of dance. Prominent
among these works are *Nigerian Dances, Four Igbo Songs, A Sketch
For Trombone,* and *Ritual Procession.* Some of the elements that
stimulate dance in Uzoigwe's music are the rhythmic structures,
accentuation of regulative beats, cyclic arrangement of piano
accompaniments, and the use of folksongs.

As Nketia explains, it is generally the rhythmic structure of music
that influences the pattern of motion (Nketia 1974:210). Uzoigwe
uses metrical rhythms to suggest dance in his music. The constant
reiteration of strong accents in linear and multilinear patterns
informs the listener on the points for changing body position. In
other words, the articulation of basic pulsations with sophisticated
rhythms stimulate dance. Uzoigwe observes the role of rhythmic

structure in *ukom* music of the Igbo. He explains that like most Igbo music, *ukom* is dance-oriented because it is essentially structured to arouse physical response by the listeners. The motoristic elements in *ukom* according to Uzoigwe are its moderate, steady tempo and vivacious rhythmic esence (Uzoigwe 1988:72). In Akan dances (*adowa* and *sikyi*), dancers are guided by the recognition and proper articulation of the basic regulative beats of the music. The basic steps of the dance divide the time line, articulated by a bell, into two or multiples of two. When it is in two divisions, the right foot moves forward on the strong beat of the pattern, followed by the left foot on the next beat-that is, the initial beat of the second half of the pattern (Nketia 1974:213).

The constant interplay of multilinear syncopated rhythmic structures is a dynamic device to stimulate dancing. This technique is observed in *A Sketch For Trombone* (measures 7 to 10), where there is a continuous interaction between the trombone line and the two hands of the piano accompaniment. The independence of the three lines due to the rhythmic disposition gives the impression of three traditional instruments playing simultaneously (see example 34).

Example 34. Syncopations in *A Sketch For Trombone* mm. 7-10

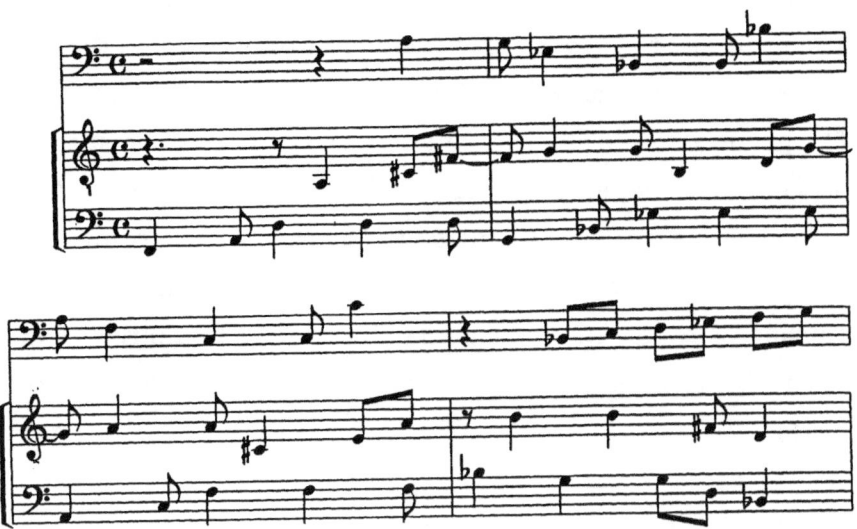

The use of a distinctive rhythmic pattern throughout a piece is another dance element in Uzoigwe's music. Usually, he will assign this rhythmic pattern to a particular part, line or instrument. Uzoigwe assigns this type of pattern to the left hand of the piano accompaniment in *Nigerian Dances No. 1,* and to a bell (metronome instrument) in *Ritual Procession.* The rhythm is expected to be played by the bell throughout the entire piece. This same principle guides the use of the *ogene* (large metal bell) in the traditional *atilogwu* dance of the Igbo, where the bell echoes or delineates the rhythm of the footwork (ibid.:212). See example 22 for the rhythmic pattern of the bell in *Ritual Procession.*

Another rhythmic device that suggests dance in Uzoigwe's music is the ostinato patterns. The continuous repetition of specific melo/rhythmic patterns in the *Nigerian Dances* can influence the listener to dance. What excites motion in the listener is the regular interplay of the constant (ostinato) and the variable (melodic line). The juxtaposition of the two lines creates an irresistible stimulus to dance. This experience is similar to the technique of Uzoigwe's piano accompaniments to the *Four Igbo Songs*. The cyclic arrangement of the accompaniment in a quasi-ostinato style easily stimulates dancing. Also, the rhythmic interaction of the left and right hands is irresistible to dance (see example 35 for the piano accompaniment of *Tuzu*).

Example 35. Piano Accompaniment of *Tuzu*
mm. 8-11

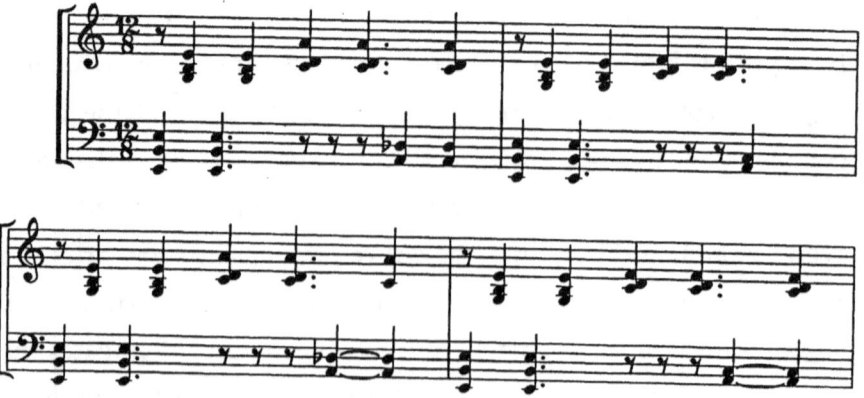

The final element of dance in Uzoigwe's music is the borrowed songs. The idea of borrowing folktunes or folksongs for composition do stimulate motion in the listeners. The recognition of a familiar tune can easily trigger the listener to tap his feet, to tap his lap with hands or to sway his head. This type of gesture is made as a form of patriotism and cultural identification. Uzoigwe's approach to the borrowing of folksongs is similar to that of European nationalist composers such as Bela Bartok and Zoltan Kodaly. *Four Igbo Songs* and *Nigerian Dances* are works with direct borrowed themes (see examples 1a, 4a, and 38a for excerpts of Nigerian folksongs in Uzoigwe's music). This concept is similar to that of the *eseni* dance of the Ijaw, in which the movements are fixed to the rhythmic lines of a song rather than the accompanying percussion, and are repeated with every repetition of the song (Nketia 1974:212). The interrelations of singing and dancing is also observed in the Ogboni and Egungun cults of the Yoruba such as *Alagbo, Sembe* and *Arebe* (Akpabot 1986:44).

From the preceeding postulations, we can assert that a great deal of dancing is inspired by distinctive musical ideations. Furthermore, the creative impulse of the dancer or listener for motion hinges on a variety of musical ideations. Whereas, he is creatively restricted with limited phrases or patterns from the music, he often falls back on his intuitive inventiveness.

Instrumentation

Interculturalism in Uzoigwe's music is quite pronounced in his integration of musical instruments from African and Western traditions. *Masquerade I* and *II*, *Eriri Ngeringe*, *Tuzu*, *Ritual Procession* and *Watermaid* are works in which he conjoins musical instruments from the two cultures. *Masquerade I* and *II* is a work for piano and Yoruba talking drum, the *iyaalu*. However, the role assigned to the *iyaalu* in *Masquerade I* (ostinato pattern) is contrary to its traditional role. In a typical *dundun* ensemble, it is the secondary drums that play the repeated patterns, while the *iyaalu* plays the improvisatory section. Uzoigwe's technique may be referred to as a recreation of tradition in a contemporary sense. In *Eriri Ngeringe*, and *Tuzu*, he merely assigned a specific rhythmic pattern to maracas to serve as background accompaniment for the songs. Similarly, Uzoigwe assigned a definite rhythmic pattern to *ogene* (metal bell) in *Ritual Procession* and to a woodblock in *Watermaid* (First and final movements).

It must be stressed that Uzoigwe composes essentially for Western musical instruments such as the piano and orchestra. However, he manipulates Western instruments to evoke African traditional musical instruments. For example, Uzoigwe adopts Western flute to imitate the Igbo local flute, *oja*, and the bassoon to imitate the Yoruba talking drum (*iyaalu*) in *Oja*.

In addition, all the wind instruments in *Ritual Procession* such as flute, oboe, clarinet and bassoon, are given specific melo/rhythmic patterns to imitate Nigerian traditional musical instruments.

Titles of Works

In order to fully comprehend the cultural roots of Uzoigwe's music, we may need to examine the significance of titles he gave them. Titles such as the *Nigerian Dances*, the *Talking Drums, Masquerades* and the *Ritual Procession*, portray distinctive symbolic elements. For instance, in the *Talking Drums*, Uzoigwe uses dissonant figurations and rhythmic structures to simulate the percussive strokes of the Yoruba talking drum, the *iyaalu*. The *Ritual Procession* is a musical painting of an Igbo traditional ritual ceremony. In this work, Uzoigwe attempts to evoke "total art." In African traditional ceremonies, music is seldom performed in isolation, nor is dance staged without music. A typical traditional ceremony would feature music, dance, poetry and mime. The regular juxtaposition of the various arts leads to the conclusion that African theater is "total theater" and that African art is "total art" (Euba 1988:58). To reinforce this assertion, Uzoigwe describes *ukom* music as a cultural subsystem that reflects a synthesis of other Igbo creative arts such as language, drama, dance, and perhaps, to a lesser degree, the visual arts (Uzoigwe 1988:71). Thus, the titles of Uzoigwe's music reveal that the works were not conceived as 'absolute music,' but took bearing from socio-cultural activities. Such titles invariably create a psychic picture of the music in the performer.

The titles of Uzoigwe's music served as impetus for inspiration and imagination. One might assert that the titles of the works have a great impact on the shape and stylistic features of the music. The creative imagination of Uzoigwe must have been influenced in one way or the other by the titles of the works; irrespective of which one came first, the music or the title.

The traditional and Western sources exemplified in Uzoigwe's music vividly place his works in the realm of modern African musical genres. His imagination is often ignited by African traditional and Western musical principles. Suffice it to say that, Uzoigwe's works are a good representation of intercultural music. He successfully integrates African and Western musical idioms to create his own style of modern African art music. The intercultural aspect of Uzoigwe's music lies not only in the instrumentation or the component materials, but in the composer's conception and in his method of integrating African and European elements.

CHAPTER 5

CONCLUSION

The study of Uzoigwe's life and music has illustrated the impact of European missionization and colonisation on the emergence of modern African art music. Colonial education enhanced the spirit of nationalism rather than totally Westernizing the African elite. The introduction of Western music notation, instruments and genres, has enabled and equipped Africans to partake in the global creative exercise of intercultural music. Uzoigwe, like other composers of contemporary African art music, such as Fela Sowande (Nigeria), Ayo Bankole (Nigeria), Ephraim Amu (Ghana), Kwabena Nketia (Ghana), Solomon Mbabi-Katana (Uganda), Gamal Abdel-Rahim (Egypt), and Halim El-Dabh (Egypt) is a modern interculturalist.

The music of Sowande is based on both Western and African indigenous techniques. Many of his themes are derivations of Nigerian traditional music. Works such as *Oyigiyigi* (organ), *Obangiji* (organ), *African Suite For Strings* and *A Folk Symphony* (full orchestra) are all based on African/Nigerian musical elements. Sowande's concept of derivative materials is much broader than Uzoigwe's in that his themes reflect both African and African American idioms as seen in his arrangements of spirituals (*Wheel, Oh Wheel, Roll de Chariot, Stan' Still Jordan* etc). Sowande's style of composition belongs more to the Romantic and early modern tradition (Baker 1978:137).

Ayo Bankole, until his tragic death in 1976 was one of the most prolific Nigerian modern composers. His training in Western music at the Guildhall School of Music, London, and at the University of Cambridge, England, and ethnomusicology at the University of California, Los Angeles, is vividly manifest in his works. Bankole belongs to the next generation of composers after Sowande, thus, his creative style is a step further from Sowande's. Bankole's studies in ethnomusicology influenced his compositions and among the works of his UCLA period were *Ethnophony* and *Jonas,* a cantata for soloists, chorus and a mixed ensemble including African instruments and the Indian *tambura.* While studying in the United Kingdom and the United States of America, Bankole employed various twentieth-century Western techniques in his work (such as the twelve-tone technique), but on his return to Nigeria in 1966, he simplified his idiom, in order to make local performances of his music possible and his work approachable to Nigerian audiences. Other notable works by Bankole are *Cantata No.4, Festac* for soloists, chorus and mixed ensemble of Western and African instruments, *Sonata No.2 in C, The Passion* for piano, *Three Part-Songs,* for female choir and *Three Toccatas* for organ etc. (Euba 1993:12,46).

Amu shows a preference for the vocal medium, although he has composed for both Western and African instruments. In some of his music, African scales and harmonies prevail, while in other music, Western styles of major and minor tonalities appear.

Similar to Sowande, Amu's style of composition shares affinity with the Baroque and Romantic tradition of Western music. Among Amu's works are *Ten Vocal Pieces, Wo Nsam Mewo, Enne Ye Anigyeda, Two Pieces for Bamboo Flute and Piano* etc... (Baker 1978:132,133).

According to Euba (1993:15-16, 50-51), Kwabena Nketia's work exemplifies the concept of creative ethnomusicology.[1] His idiom is based on the pre-twentieth century Western practice and 'dissonance' is almost totally absent from his music. The harmonic idiom of Amu and Nketia show a peculiarly Ghanaian progression, although derived from Western chords (ibid.:16). Nketia, like Bartok, has successfully translated the results of his research into an original creative idiom and a study of his music will provide an insight into the processes that lead from analysis back to synthesis (ibid.:16). Some of Nketia's works are *A Widow's Prayer* for flute and piano, *Antubam* for cello and piano, *Apranaa Sa Me* for voice and piano, *Atenteben:* Tunes for Bamboo flutes, *Dargati March* for piano, *Volta Fantasy* for piano and *Yen Agoro Yi* for unaccompanied male choir.

Another African composer with a strong ethnomusicological background is Solomon Mbabi-Katana. Although he has composed for the piano, his main achievement is in the exploration of the use of African traditional instruments in modern composition. His works, like Nketia's, are a direct result of ethnomusicological research.

---

[1] Creative ethnomusicology is the creative application of ethnomusicological methods. It is the practice whereby an investigator goes beyond analysis and uses information derived from analysis as the basis of creative work (Euba No.2 1989:122).

Mbabi-Katana's *Midday Dream* shares affinity with Uzoigwe's *Ritual Procession* in terms of structure and instrumentation. The *Midday Dream* is a three-movement work scored for an ensemble of African instruments, comprising wood block, cow bells, small drum, big drum, rattle, xylophone, bow lutes, thumb pianos, pan pipes and slit drum. The composer, like Uzoigwe in his *Ritual Procession,* provides copious notes in the score describing the instruments and how they are played. The notion of neo-African ensemble, such as Mbabi-Katana's, implies the combination of musical instruments drawn from different ethnic sources. Other works by Mbabi-Katana are *Akogo Dance* for piano, *Irambi* for piano and *The Marriage of Nyakato,* an opera (Euba 1993:15,49).

Abdel-Rahim's work shows a long search for an individual style fusing essentially oriental modal and rhythmic features with modern Western techniques. His melodies are always modal, and intervals characteristic of Arab music--the augmented 2nd of *hijaz,* the diminished 4th of *saba*--are prevalent. Egyptian elements also characterise his harmony and polyphonic writing, while his rhythm combines traditional irregular patterns (groups of five, seven etc) with Western variable meters. His use of sonata form in his Violin Sonata, displays some novel details, stimulated by eastern improvisation, as means of contrast in the second subject. Abdel-Rahim belongs to the second generation of Egyptian nationalist composers.

His melodies are usually recreations of folk music rather than direct quotations, except in some variation sets. Some of his works are *Variations on an Egyptian Folktune* (piano), *The Sinai Epic* (orchestra), and *Erwachen*, a cantata for baritone, choir and orchestra (El Kholy 1980:8).

The music of Halim El-Dabh, another Egyptian composer, is colored by African and Egyptian elements, for which he has evolved a special notation. The writing is frequently monodic, with unusual rhythms and percussive devices that lend it an exotic and often archaic quality. The Egyptian/African aspects of El-Dabh's music are boldly realized and are evident in (a) the tonal and rhythmic style (b) the choice of instruments and (c) the choice of title and/or subject matter. Among his pieces for piano is *Mekta in the Art of Kita,* books I and II, whose title may be translated as "The Microcosm in the Art of Macrocosm." Other piano works by El-Dabh include 25 *Arabiyaats* (Arabic forms), 25 *Misriyaats* (Egyptian forms), and 25 *Ifrigiyaats* (African forms). *Clytemnestra* is an epic dance-drama for dancers, intoned voices (dramatic soprano and dramatic baritone with falsetto range) and orchestra (Euba 1989:139,140).

Uzoigwe's works like those of other African composers mentioned above, are based on the syncretization of the African and Western musical idioms. As Nketia observes, the development of a cross-cultural perspective can enable African composers to draw on a wide range of resources over and above those of their ethnic groups (Nketia 1995:230). The influence of the serial composers

(Schoenberg, Berg and Webern) Uzoigwe studied while at the Guildhall School of Music, London, can be seen in the twelve-tone technique employed in his works such as *Oja* and *Sketches* for Piano. Uzoigwe belongs to the twentieth-century school of intercultural composers. He successfully conjoins creative techniques of his tradition with modern Western devices. Some of the Africanisms in Uzoigwe's music include choice of indigenous scales (particularly Igbo), form, intervallic structures, rhythms, element of dance, local themes, instrumentation and title of works.

The analysis of Uzoigwe's music shows that this music (like Nketia's, Bankole's and Mbabi-Katana's), is a product of ethnomusicological research. The influence of Uzoigwe's extensive research on *ukom* music is evident in his composition particularly the *Ritual Procession* and *Oja*. From the preceding argument, Uzoigwe is not only an interculturalist, but also a creative ethnomusicologist. He has been able to transcend the level of borrowing traditional themes to that of recreation of indigenous musical elements and applying the result to his work. As Nketia has shown, modern African composers must be able, for example, to invent an original tune or rhythm pattern that is idiomatic in African tradition. This demands deeper familiarity with an African musical language and its idioms. For one needs to know not just what kind of scales and modes are used but also the manner in which the constituent notes are ordered in units of structure and the intervals that clarify their relationship (Nketia 1995:227).

The piano works of Uzoigwe are characterised by the elements of 'African pianism.'[2] Nketia (1994:iii) describes 'African pianism' as a style of piano music which derives its characteristic idiom from the procedures of African percussion music exemplified in bell patterns, drumming, xylophone and mbira music. Elements of 'African pianism' in Uzoigwe's keyboard music, for example *Nigerian Dances, Sketches, Lustra Variations, Four Igbo Songs* (piano accompaniment), and the *Talking Drum* are the use of indigenous rhythmic motifs, themes of traditional songs, percussive treatment of the piano and the evocation of African instruments. Euba likewise notes that the piano accompaniment in the first of Uzoigwe's *Four Igbo Songs* for voice and piano clearly demonstrates the concept of African pianism. The piano is made to 'behave' like an African instrument and the piano part sounds as if it were a transcription of an African instrumental part rather than a through-composed part (Euba 1993:20).

The pronounced influence of African traditional music on Uzoigwe's works is due to the following factors. First, Uzoigwe's contact with the works of Nigerian modern composers, while at the International School, Ibadan, was very crucial to his creative career. By studying and performing such works, he acquired knowledge on how to recombine Nigerian traditional musical resources to create modern compositions. Second, the civil war was a turning point for Uzoigwe's ethnic identity. The war made him aware and proud of being an

---

[2] The concept of 'African pianism' was pioneered by Akin Euba (see for example Euba 1993:8).

Igbo, hence the *Four Igbo Songs*. Third, the spirit of nationalism which followed the independence of Nigeria trigerred his search for an African identity and audience. This he achieved by employing musical elements not only from the Igbo, but also from other ethnic groups such as the Yoruba (for instance, in the *Nigerian Dances*). The fourth and final reason for the pronounced influence of African traditional music on Uzoigwe's works is the study of ethnomusicology at Belfast. Studying ethnomusicology opened his eyes to the creative principles of indigenous African music. Through various research activities, he has been able to extract creative techniques from traditional sources and apply them to his works.

The new art music of Africa represents a departure from and reodering of traditional creative techniques. Moreover, it implies the development of new social contexts for music. The question then arises, who are the patrons that constitute the audience for this music? The audiences of Uzoigwe's music belong to certain segment of the Nigerian elite--upper-middle-class, intellectuals, students and the affluent. To the knowledge of the author, the *Four Igbo Songs, Nigerian Dances* for piano and the *Talking Drum* are the most popular among the Nigerian audiences.[3] These works have been well received because the audiences have been able to relate to the Africanisms (especially the folktunes and rhythms) in the works. For illustration, the author observed a wonderful reception of these

---

[3] Other works by Uzoigwe are unpopular because they are either too difficult for performers to play or sing or the facilities are not there to perform them. For example, apart from *Fanfare* for brass ensemble, none of his orchestral works have been performed in Nigeria due to the none availability of standard orchestra in the country.

genres by the audience at the inaugural conference of the Musicological Society of Nigeria, in 1993, at the University of Ilorin. Uzoigwe himself performed the three works mentioned above. The audience demonstrated their appreciation for the music by humming some of the well known folktunes in the *Nigerian Dances Nos. 2,3 and 4*, and the *Four Igbo Songs*. Another form of identification with these works by the audience was through the swaying of their body, tapping of feet and hand clapping in response to the irresistible rhythmic structures of the music. The rhythms stimulated dance in the audience. A performance such as this inevitably creates a psychomotor effect in the audience, thus, communication takes place. In order to bring the music closer to its African roots, Uzoigwe assigned the *konkonkolo* rhythm (or the West African time line--see example 24 in chapter 4) to a wood clapper to accompany the last piece in the *Nigerian Dances* and the *Talking Drum*. This novel effort earned him a standing ovation and an encore. The author has similarly performed these works at public concerts and recitals in different parts of Nigeria and has received good responses from the audiences because of the aforementioned reasons.

Uzoigwe is not exempted from one of the critical problems confronting modern African composers, that is, the traces of Western hegemony that pervade their works. At the conceptual level, Uzoigwe's compositions have their strongest roots in African traditional background, but his mode of realizing them, in terms of tonal organization and instrumentation, suggests European musical influence.

In other words, at the point of conception, Uzoigwe is thinking African, but the final output exhibits Western influence. As Uzoigwe himself explains,

> this (problem) is due to the fact that, at the point of material construction or creative synthesis of elements, Western/European musical elements such as notational and instrumental techniques, and concert-hall performance, tend as a whole to overshadow the African elements (Uzoigwe 1992b:61).

This problem could be traced back to the impact of the missionary church and schools in Nigeria, and Uzoigwe's training in Western musical tradition at the Guildhall. Up to that point, Uzoigwe was mostly exposed to European musical idioms. It is not surprising that his creative works reflect his Western training.

"Is African Music Possible?" asks Abiola Irele (1993:61-71) in a recent essay, referring mainly to African art music. The answer of this author to Irele's question is in the affirmative; yes, African art music is possible. There has been an aggresive dissemination of this genre in the last decade by professionally trained Nigerian composers, performers, musicologists and amateur musicians. The last decade has witnessed tremendous performances of this genre by the Ife Choral Society, Terra Chorale, Department of Music (all based in the Obafemi Awolowo University, Ife-Ife), Music Society of Nigeria, Music Circle, Laz Ekwueme Chorale and the Nigerian Association of Music Educators. In fact, Euba (1988:107), notes that efforts have been made by various groups and organizations (beginning with the Lagos Musical Society in the 1940's) to promote art music in Nigeria in the last four decades. See appendix B for some concert programs by these associations in which African art music is featured.

The means of dissemination has been through regular performances of the works at public concerts, schools--secondary schools, teacher training colleges and Universities, and discussions in the form of scholarly paper presentations at conferences. For instance, the Musicological Society of Nigeria holds an annual conference in which the state of African art music is often discussed and the works performed at its concerts. One other medium of dissemination has been through weekly radio broadcast of the music at both federal and state levels. The program has always being a weekly production for short periods over the years. The broadcasts are usually aired at off-peak hours between 9:00PM and 11:00PM mostly on Sundays or during the week. A short biography of the composers and information on their musical styles preceds the playing of the music in order to serve as background knowledge for the audiences.

Another dimension is the launching (in 1987) by the West African Examination Council of a new syllabus for music in the prospectus of the West African Schools' Certificate. The new syllabus incorporates for the first time ever the study of modern art music by African composers. The new syllabus opens up an important avenue for the study, understanding and promotion of modern African art music and, by bringing this music into the schools' curriculum, provides one of the structures necessary for a wide-ranging dissemination of the genre (Euba 1988:108,109). The Department of Music, Obafemi Awolowo University, Ile-Ife, has also followed this trend. In the department, it is mandatory for students specialising in performance (voice or piano) to include a work by a modern African composer in their repertoire.[4]   There is no doubt that there is a bright future for modern African art music considering the strategies mounted by its practitioners to bring awareness of it to the larger society. The new developments over the last decade show convincingly that composers of African art music such as Uzoigwe may soon receive the kind of national and international recognition that they deserve.

---

[4] The author's graduation piano recital in the same department in 1988 included works by Johann Sebastian Bach, Ludwig Van Beethoven, Fryderyk Chopin, Claude Debussy and Joshua Uzoigwe.

APPENDICES

APPENDIX A

List of Compositions by Joshua Uzoigwe

Below is a selected list of works by Joshua Uzoigwe. The date of completion of works is given at the end of each piece.

Solo Voice and Accompaniment

1. *Four Igbo Songs* (1973)

    (i) "Eriri Ngeringe" for mezzo soprano and piano

    (ii) "Uyaroma" for mezzo soprano and piano

    (iii) "Ite Etipia Etipia" for mezzo soprano and piano

    (iv) "Tuzu" for mezzo soprano and piano

2. *Watermaid* for voice solo and orchestra (1984)

Choral Works

3. *Sirene Limits* for *a capella* choir SATB (1976)

4. *Grand Little One* SATB and piano (1976)

5. *Two Songs* for Mixed Chorus (1976)

Solo Instrument and Accompaniment

6. *Masquerade I and II* for iyaalu drum and piano (1979)

7. *A Sketch for Trombone* and piano (1986)

Quartet

8. *Oja* for Wind Quartet (1978)

Orchestra/Symphony

9. *Nigerian Dances* for chamber orchestra (1976)

10. *Lustra Variations* for symphony orchestra (1978)

11. *Ritual Procession* for African/European orchestra (1978)

12. *Fanfare* for Brass Ensemble (1981)

Piano Solo

13. *Nigerian Dances* for piano (1977)

14. *Lustra Variations* for piano (1977)

15. *Sketches* for piano (1977)

16. *The Talking Drum* for piano (1991)

APPENDIX B

Concert Programs

Find below concert programs showing performances of works by modern African art music composers. Notice the consistency of cross-cultural musical repertoire--African and Western pieces. The concert program below was organized by the Music Circle of the University of Ibadan.

PROGRAMME

Gretchen am Spinnrade (*Margaret at the Spinning Wheel*) — Schubert
Auf Dem Wasser zu Singen — Schubert
[To be sung on the waters]
If Its Ever Spring Again — Christopher le Fleming
Die Forelle (*The Trout*) — Schubert

Yemisi Adewoye — Soprano
Amorelle Inanga — Piano

Sonata in F Op. 10 No. 2 — Beethoven
Allegro
Allegretto
Presto
Wakar Duru — Akin Euba

Godwin Sadoh — Piano

Tom Der Reimer — Loewe
Recit: Che Mai Vegg'io! — Verdi
Aria: Infelice!
(Ernani)
Am I Alone and Unobserved? — Sullivan
(Patience)

Michael Hudson — Baritone
Amorelle Inanga — Piano

Impromptus — Schubert
Op. 90 No. 3 G Flat Major
Op. 142 No. 4 in F Minor
Edward Boamah — Piano

INTERVAL 15 MINUTES

Sento Nel Core — Alessandro Scarlatti
The Turtle Dove — arranged by Laz Ekwueme
O Sumoti Kwikelo (*He-goat go back*)
Alago's Song, Plateau State — arranged by Okechukwu Ndubuisi
Three Igbo Songs — Laz Ekwueme
  i. Oge (*Time*)
  ii. Nne, bia Nyerem aba (*Mother, please help*)
  iii. Elimeli (*Festal day*)

Laz Ekwueme — Tenor
Richard Bucknor — Piano

Sonata in D major "Pastoral" Op. 28 — Beethoven
Allegro
Andante
Allegro Vivace
Allegro Ma Non Troppo
Edward Boamah — Piano

Aria: Say Goodbye Now to Pastime — Mozart
  (The Marriage of Figaro)
Recit: A te L'Estremo Addio — Verdi
Aria: Il Lacerato Spirito
  (Simon Boccanegra)
The Vagabond — Vaughan-Williams
Ise Oluwa — arranged by Olu Sowande

Christopher Oyesiku — Bass
Amorelle Inanga — Piano

The concert below was organized by the Musicological Society of Nigeria as part of the closing ceremony for its inaugural conference on Nigerian Music. The concert took place on January 1st, 1993, at the Courtyard of the Department of Performing Arts, University of Ilorin.

- 2 -

Programme

) National Anthem : --	by Ben Odiase, Arr. Bode Omojola
) UNILORIN ANTHEM -	words by Adavi, music by Odejimi
) Emi yio Gbe Oju mi soke -	by T.K.E. Phillips
: Ajamakwari ngwo ngwo	(I shall carry my property - by Okechukwu Ndubuisi
, Ka jo jo -	by Yemi Olaniyan

:versity of Ilorin choir

:st conductor: A. K. Achinivu
:ompanist: Bode Omojola

, Danso Danso -	Godwin Sadoh
, Wakar Duru -	Akin Euba
(1st and 2nd movement)	

!win Sadoh: Piano

) Mawue Naa wue -	E. Amu
) Bonwere Kentenwene-	E. Amu
, Babalawo Ma'wa bebe-	J. Olubobokun
, Ore meta -	Akin Euba
funmi Boamah -	Soprano
Edward Boamah -	Piano/Accompanist
Kale -	K. Kafui
Divine presence -	A. A. Mensah

- 3 -

| Edward Boamah: | Piano |

5.(a) Three	-	Joshua Uzoigwe
.(b) Ha ya aka	-	Joshua Uzoigwe
(c) Diyaroma	-	Joshua Uzoigwe

Joyce Adewumi: Soprano
Joshua Uzoigwe: Piano/Accompanist

6.   Nigerian Dances (a suite): Joshua Usoigw
Talking Drums (3 movements):Joshua Uzoig
Joshua Uzoigwe: Piano

| 7.(a) Because - | - by Guy D'Hardelot |
| (b) Pace, Pace, mio Dio-by Giuseppe Verdi |
| (c) Uwam | - by Joy Nwosu Lo Bami |

Joy Nwosu Lo Bamijoko: Soprano
Richard Bucknor: Piano Accompanis

8.(a) Ona kan	-	by Bode Omojola
(b) Gbo ohun	-	Arr. Sam Amusan
(c) Supplication	-	by Adolf Ahanotu
(d) Anyi buihe	-	by Ikoli Harcoourt Wohyte
(e) Afebi G'adi	-	by A.K. Achinivu
(f) National Anthem	-	by Ben Odiase, Arr. Bode Omojola

University of Ilorin choir

Guest Conductor: -   A. K. Achinivu
Piano/Accompanist   -   Bode Omojola

THANK YOU FOR YOUR SPONSORSHIP AND
FOR APPRECIATING US.

DIRECTOR.

Find below one of the annual Christmas concert programs by the Choral Society of the Obafemi Awolowo University, Ile-Ife. The venue was Saint Paul's Anglican Church, Aiyegbaju, Ile-Ife, on December 16th, 1992.

PROGRAMME

```
    Emi yoo gbe oju mi - Ekundayo Phillips
)   Miri Ndu            - Laz Ekwueme
i)  Ise Oluwa           - Ekundayo Phillips
)   Enikeni to ba gbe ara re ga - Ayo Bankole
                                      (Snr)
              Chorus
         Organ: Bode Omojola
         Conductor: Godwin Sadoh


    I got a robe   - H.T. Burleigh
)   Tis me, O Lord - H.T. Burleigh

         Bass: Odeniyi Ayo-Ajayi
         Organ: Godwin Sadoh


Organ Recital by Christopher Ayodele


Adura fun Alafia - Ayo Bankole

         Soprano: Mojisola Abiona
         Organ: Godwin Sadoh
```

```
5(i)    Infant King - Basque Noel
 (ii)   I saw three ships - David Willcocks
 (iii)  I saw a maiden - Edgar Pettman
 (iv)   Densu, Densu/Sasa Kroma - James Yankey
              Chorus
         Organ: Bode Omojola
         Conductor: Godwin Sadoh


6(i)    Iya - Ayo Bankole
 (ii)   Ja itana to ntan - Ayo Bankole
 (iii)  Keresimesi tun ma de o - Ayo Bankole

         Bass: Idowu Abiodun
         Organ: Godwin Sadoh


7(i)    Oluwa l'oluso Agutan mi - Arr.
        Christopher Ayodele
 (ii)   Gbo Ohun Awon Angeli - Arr. Godwin Sad‹
 (iii)  Mimo mimo l'oluwa - Laz Ekwueme
 (iv)   Ding, Dong merrily on high

              Chorus
         Organ: Bode Omojola
         Conductor: Godwin Sadoh
```

Here is another concert under the auspices of the Choral Society at the Obafemi Awolowo University, Ile-Ife. The venue was the Conference Center of the same institution on July 30th, 1992.

Programme

1. (i) Emi yoo gbe oju mi s'oke — Ekundayo Phillips
   (ii) Enikeni to ba gbe aru re ga — Ayo Bankole (Snr.)
   (iii) Mimo, Mimo l'Oluwa — Anonymous
   (iv) Densu, Densu, Sansa Kroma — James Yankey

   Bethel Praise Choral — Voices
   William Plateeuw — Piano
   Oluwa Abayomi)
   Godwin Sadoh — Conductor

2. (i) Gold and Silver — Ferencz Lehar
   (ii) Allegro from Wind Sexter, Op 71 — Ludwig Beethoven
   Chijioke Ani — Clarinet
   Godwin Sadoh — Piano

3. (i) Uyaroma — Joshua Uzoigwe
   (ii) Ojo Maro — Ayo Bankole (Snr.)
   Mojisola Al... — Soprano
   Godwin Sadoh — Piano

4. Sonata in F major, KV 332 — Wolfgang Mozart
   (i) Allegro
   (ii) Adagio
   (iii) Assai Allegro
   Willem Plateeuw — Piano

5. (i) BENEDICTUS — Anonymous
   (ii) Let their Bright Seraphim — G F, Handel
   Kunbi Omideyi — Soprano
   Willem Plateeuw — Piano

6. (i) Let their Celestial Concerts all Unite — G. F. Handel
   (ii) I waited for the Lord — Felix Mendelssohn
   (iii) I am Alpha and Omega — John Stainer
   Bethel Praise Choral — Voices
   Willem Plateeuw — Piano
   Godwin Sadoh — Conductor

7. Two Pieces for Violin
   Oluwafemi Ibiayo — Violin
   Godwin Sadoh — Piano

8. (i) Arm, Arm Ye Brave — G F. Handel
   (ii) Ja Itana T'o Tan — Ayo Bankole (Snr.)
   (iii) The Flea — Modeste Moussorgski
   Ebenezer Omole — Bass
   Godwin Sadoh — Piano

9. (i) Train Blues — Christopher Norton
   (ii) Basin Street Blues — Spencer Williams arr. by Hans Heamann
   (iii) Arrival of the Queen of Sheba — G F Handel
   Godwin Sadoh — Piano Primo
   Willem Plateeuw — Piano Secondo

10. (i) Ise Oluwa — Ekundayo Phillips
    (ii) Mira Ndu — Igbo Folksong
    (iii) Akoi Wata Geri — Godwin Sadoh
    (iv) O Tete Nkwu — Lazarus Ekwueme

    Bethel Praise Choral — Voices
    Willem Plateeuw — Piano
    Oluwole Abayomi — "
    Godwin Sadoh — Conductor
    " Oluwalomoloye Bakeye — Compere

Finally, here is the program of a piano recital by this author at the Oduduwa Hall, Obafemi Awolowo University, Ile-Ife, on January 6th, 1991. Notice that the popular *Nigerian Dances* for piano solo by Joshua Uzoigwe was featured among other works.

<u>Part   One</u>

1. Minuet with Variations   — Thomas Arne
>   (i)   Theme in moderato semplice
>   (ii) Variation I
>   (iii) Poco piu mosso
>   (iv) Brillante

2. Sonata op. 14, no. 1 in E   — Ludwig Beethoven
>   (i)   Allegro
>   (ii) Allegretto
>   (iii) Maggiore
>   (iv) Rondo: Allegro Commodo

3. Deux Arabesques No.1   — Claude Debussy
4. Ballade in A Flat op. 47   — Federic Chopin

I N T E R V A L   (10 m i n u t e s)

<u>Part   Two</u>

5. Prelude in G minor, op. 23, No. 5 — S. Rachmaninoff
6. Rondo Danzo   — G. S. Sadoh
7. Nigerian Dances No. 1, 2 and 3   — J. Uzoigwe

Discography

Hollister, Darryl, 2005. *Towards an African Pianism: An Anthology of Keyboard Music from Africa and the Diaspora,* Vol. 2. Including 'Agbigbo' by Joshua Uzoigwe. CD. A Bridge Across: ABA 0001.

Inanga, Glen, 2005. *Towards an African Pianism: An Anthology of Keyboard Music from Africa and the Diaspora,* Vol. 1. Including 'Lustra Variations' by Joshua Uzoigwe. CD. A Bridge Across: ABA 0001.

Nyaho, William Chapman, 2003. *Senku: Piano Music by Composers of African Descent.* Including 'Ukom,' 'Ilulu,' and 'Egwu Amala,' from Joshua Uzoigwe's *Talking Drum.* CD. Musicians Showcase Recordings (MSR Classics). MS 1091.

BIBLIOGRAPHY

Bibliography

Achinivu, Kanu. "Ikoli Harcourt Whyte, The Man and His Music: A Case of Musical Acculturation in Nigeria." *Ethnomusikologie* 2 vols., No.7, 1979.

Adedeji, J. A. "Trends in the Content and Form of the Opening Glee in Yoruba Drama." *Research in African Literatures* vol.4, No.1, 1973.

Adegbite, Ademola. "Traditional Music in Yorubaland." Unpublished M.A. Thesis, University of Pittsburgh, 1974.

Agawu, Kofi. "Impact of Language on Musical Composition in Ghana: An Introduction to the Style of Ephraim Amu." *Ethnomusicology* vol.27, No.1, 1984.

Ajayi, Ade. J. F. *Christian Missions in Nigeria 1841-1891.* London: Longman, 1965.

Akpabot, Samuel. "The Talking Drums of Nigeria." *African Music* vol.5, No.4, 1975/76.

_____. *Foundation of Nigerian Traditional Music.* Ibadan: Spectrum Books Limited,1986.

Alaja-Browne, Afolabi. "Ayo Bankole: His Life And Works." Unpublished M.A. Thesis, University of Pittsburgh, 1981.

_____. "A History of Intercultural Art Music in Nigeria." In *Intercultural Music* vol.1, edited by Cynthia Tse Kimberlin and Akin Euba. Bayreuth: Bayreuth African Studies Series, No.29, 1995.

Anku, William. "Towards a Cross-Cultural Theory of African Rhythm: A Compositional Process." In *Intercultural Music* vol.1, edited by Cynthia Tse Kimberlin and Akin Euba. Bayreuth: Bayreuth African Studies Series, No.29, 1995.

Appadurai, Arjun. "Disjuncture and Difference in the Global Cultural Economy." *Public Lecture* vol.2, No.2, 1990.

126

Babalola, Adeboye. "Ijala Poetry Among the Oyo-Yoruba Communities." In *Oral Poetry in Nigeria,* edited by Uchegbulam N. Abalogu, Dr. Garba Ashiwaju and Regina Amadi-Tshiwala. Lagos: Nigeria Magazine, 1981.

Baker, David., et al., eds. *The Black Composer Speaks.* Metuchen, N. J.: The Scarecrow Press, 1977.

Bateye, Oluwalomoloye Oladipo. " Fiberesima, Adam: The Contemporary Nigerian Composer." Unpublished M.A. Thesis, University of Ibadan, 1982.

Beier, Ulli. "Yoruba Folk Operas." *African Music* vol.1, No.1., 1954.

Bent, Ian and William Drabkin. *Analysis.* New York: W. W. Norton, 1987.

Bent, Ian. *Music Analysis in the Nineteenth Century.* London: Cambridge University Press, 1994.

Benward, Bruce and Gary White. *Music in Theory and Practice.* New York: Brown and Beach Mark, 1977.

Blacking, John. *How Musical Is Man?* Seattle: University of Washington Press, 1973.

Carrol, Rev. Father K. "Yoruba Religious Music." *African Music* Vol.1, No.3, 1956.

Coleman, James. *Nigeria: Background to Nationalism.* Berkeley: University of California Press, 1958.

Cowell, Henry. "The Composers World." In *The Preservation of the Traditional Forms of the Learned and Popular Music of the Orient and the Occident,* edited by William Kay Archer. Urbana: Institute of Communication Research, 1961.

Crowder, Michael. *A Short History of Nigeria.* New York: Frederick A. Praeger, 1962.

Dada, S.A. *A History of the African Church.* Ibadan: Aowa Printers & Publishers, 1986.

Dallin, Leon. *Techniques of Twentieth Century Composition.* Dubuque: W.M.C. Company Publishers, 1974.

Daniel, Oliver. "El-Dabh, Halim," in *The New Grove Dictionary of Music and Musicians* 6, edited by Stanley Sadie. London: Macmillan, 1980.

Dixon, P.A.F. "Uzoigwe, Joshua." In *Contemporary Composers,* edited by Brian Morton and Pamela Collins. Chicago and London: Saint James' Press, 1992.

Dusgate, Richard. *The Conquest of Northern Nigeria.* Britain: Frank Cass & Co. Ltd., 1985.

Ekwueme, Lazarus. "African Music in Christian Liturgy: The Igbo Experiment." *African Music* vol.5, No.3, 1973/74.

_____. "Concepts of African Music Theory." *Journal of Black studies* vol.5, No.7, 1974.

_____. "Structural Levels of Rhythm and Form in African Music, with Particular Reference to the West Coast." *African Music* vol.5, No.4, 1975/76.

_____. "Analysis and Analytic Techniques in African Music: A Theory of Melodic Scales." *African Music* vol.6, No.1, 1980.

El-Kholy, Samha. "Abdel-Rahim, Gamal." In *The New Grove Dictionary of Music And Musicians,* edited by Stanley Sadie. London: Macmillan, 1980.

El-Kholy, Samha. "Gamal Abdel-Rahim's Approach to Intercultural Music." In *Intercultural Music* vol.1, edited by Cynthia Tse Kimberlin and Akin Euba. Bayreuth: Bayreuth African Studies Series, No.29, 1995.

El-Kholy, Samha and John Robison. eds. *Festschrift for Gamal Abdel-Rahim.* Cairo: Bi-National Fulbright Commission, 1994.

Euba, Akin. "Traditional Elements as the Basis of New African Art Music." *African Notes* vol.5, No.4, 1970.

_____. *Essays on Music in Africa* 1, Bayreuth: Iwalewa Haus, 1988.

_____. *Essays on Music in Africa* 2: *Intercultural Perspectives.* Lagos and Bayreuth: Elekoto Music Center & Bayreuth African Studies, 1989.

_____. "Yoruba Music in the Church: The Development of a Neo- African Art Among the Yoruba of Nigeria." In *African Musicology: Current Trends* vol.2, edited by Jacqueline Cogdell DjeDje and William G. Carter. Atlanta, GA: Crossroads Press, 1989.

_____. *Yoruba Drumming: The Dundun Tradition.* Bayreuth: Eckhard Breitinger, 1990.

_____. "Creating Authentic Forms of New African Art Music." Unpublished paper presented at the International Conference on *African Music and Dance: Problems and Prospects,* at the Rockefeller Foundation Center, Bellagio, Italy, No.7,1992.

_____. *Modern African Music.* Bayreuth: Iwalewa-Haus, 1993.

_____. "Neo-African Art Music and Jazz: Related Paths." *International Jazz Archive Journal* vol.1, No.1, 1994.

Fika, Adamu M. *The Kano Civil War and British Over-Rule 1882-1940.* Ibadan: Oxford University Press, 1978.

Green, Douglas. *Form in Tonal Music.* New York: Holt, Rinehart & Winston, 1979.

Griffiths, Paul. *Bartok.* London: J.M. Dent & Sons Limited, 1984.

Hood, Mantle. "The Challenge of Bi-Musicality." *Ethnomusicology* vol.4, No.2, 1960.

Irele, Abiola. "Is African Music Possible?" *Transition* No.61, 1993.

Isichei, Elizabeth. *Varieties of Christian Experiences in Nigeria.* London: Macmillan Press, 1982.

_____. *A History of Nigeria.* London: Longman, 1983.

Jeyifo, Biodun. *The Truthful Lie: Essays in a Sociology of African Drama.* London: New Beacon Books, 1985.

Jones, A. M. *African Hymnody in Christian Worship: A Contribution to the History of its Development.* Rhodesia: Mambo Press, 1976.

Khos, Ellis. *Musical Form: Studies in Analysis & Synthesis.* Boston: Hougton Mifflin Co., 1976.

Kirby, Percival. "The Changing Face of African Music South of the Zambezi." In *Essays on Music and History in Africa,* edited by Klaus P. Wachsmann. Evanston: Northwestern University Press, 1971.

Kostka, Stefan and Dorothy Payne. *Tonal Harmony.* New York: Alfred A. Knopf, 1989.

LaRue, Jan. *Guidelines for Style Analysis.* Michigan: Harmonie Park Press, 1992.

Lesznai, Lajos. *Bartok.* London: J.M. Dent & Sons Limited, 1973.

Lomax, Alan. *Cantometrics: A Method in Musical Anthropology.* Berkeley, California: University of California, Extension Media Center, 1976.

Louw, Johan. "The Use of African Music in the Church." *African Music* vol.1, No.3, 1956.

Lurry, Rev. Canon E.E. "Music in African Churches." *African Music* vol.1, No.3, 1956.

Machlis, Joseph. *Introduction to Contemporary Music.* New York: W. W. Norton & Company, 1979.

Mackay, Mercedes, and Augustine Ene. "Atilogwu." *African Music,* vol.1, No.4, 1957.

Mckay, George. *Creative Orchestration.* Boston: Allyn and Bacon Inc., 1969.

Mensah, Atta Annan. "The Arts of Africa: Dawn or Twilight." In *African Musicology: Current Trends* vol.2, edited by Jacqueline Cogdell DjeDje and William Carter. Atlanta, GA: Crossroads Press, 1989.

Musa, Isaac. "Euba, Akin." In *Contemporary Composers,* edited by Brian Morton and Pamela Collins. Chicago and London: Saint James' Press, 1992.

New Grove Dictionary of Music and Musicians 17, "Sowande, Fela." edited by Stanley Sadie. London: Macmillan, 1980.

Nketia, Kwabena. "The Contribution of African Culture to Christian Worship." In *The Church in Changing Africa.* New York: International Missionary Council, 1958.

_____. *The Music of Africa.* New York: W.W. Norton,1974.

_____. "Developing Contemporary Idioms Out of Traditional Music." *Studia Musicologica Scientiarum Hungaricae* vol.24, 1982.

_____. *African Pianism: Twelve Pedagogical Pieces.* Accra: Afram Publications Limited, 1994.

_____. "Exploring African Musical Resources in Contemporary Compositions." In *Intercultural Music* vol.1, edited by Cynthia Tse Kimberlin and Akin Euba. Bayreuth: African Studies Series, No.29, 1995.

Nzewi, Meki. *Musical Practice and Creativity.* Bayreuth: Iwalewa-Haus, 1991.

Ohadike, Don C. *The Ekumekwu Movement.* Athens: Ohio University Press, 1991.

Olaniyan, Richard, ed. *Nigerian History and Culture.* New York: Longman, 1985.

Omibiyi, Mosunmola. "The Process of Education and the Search for Identity in Contemporary African Music." In *African Musicology: Current Trends* vol.2, edited by Jacqueline Cogdell DjeDje and William G. Carter. Atlanta, GA: Crossroads Press, 1989.

_____. "Issues in the Study of Contemporary African Art Music in Nigeria." Unpublished paper presented at the International Conference on *African Music and Dance* at the Rockefeller Foundation Center, Bellagio, Italy, No.7, 1992.

Omojola, Bode. *Nigerian Art Music: with an Introductory Study of Ghanaian Art Music.* Ibadan: Institut Francais de Recherche en Afrique, 1995.

Omoyajowo, Akinyele. *Cherubim and Seraphim.* U.S.A.: Nok Publishers, 1982.

Parrinder, E. G. "Music in West African Churches." *African Music* vol.1, No.3, 1956.

Peil, Margaret. *Lagos: The City is the People.* London: Belhaven Press, 1991.

Persichetti, Vincent. *Twentieth-Century Harmony: Creative Aspects and Practice.* New York: W.W. Norton, 1961.

Robison, John O. "The Chamber Music of Gamal Adel-Rahim and the Fusion of Traditional Egyptian and Western Elements in Modern Egyptian Music." In *Intercultural Music* vol.1, edited by Cynthia Tse Kimberlin and Akin Euba. Bayreuth: Bayreuth African Studies Series, No.29, 1995.

Saro-Wiwa, Ken. *On a Darkling Plain: An Account of the Nigerian Civil War.* London: Saros International Publishers, 1989.

Shaffer, Jacqueline. "Experiments in Indigenous Music Among the Batetela." *African Music* vol.1, No.3, 1956.

Soyinka, Wole, and LeRoi Jones. *Theater and Nationalism.* Ile-Ife: University of Ife Press, 1983.

Stein, R. *Creativity and Culture.* Journal of *Psychology* vol. 36, No.7,1953.

Stevens, Halsey. *The Life and Music of Bela Bartok.* London: Oxford University Press, 1964.

Tovey, Donald F. *Essay in Musical Analysis.* London: Oxford University Press, 1935.

Travis, Roy. "Traditional Ashanti Dances as a Compositional Resource: Tachema-Chema and Sikyi." In *Intercultural Music* vol.1, edited by Cynthia Tse Kimberlin and Akin Euba. Bayreuth: Bayreuth African Studies Series, No.29, 1995.

Turkson, Adolphus R. "Contrafactum and Parodied Song Texts in Religious Music: A Discussion of Problems and Challenges in Contemporary African Music." In *African Musicology: Current Trends* vol.2, edited by Jacqueline Cogdell DjeDje and William Carter. Atlanta, GA: Crossroads Press, 1992.

Turner, Harold. W. *History of an African Independent Church.* Oxford: Clarendon Press, 1967.

Turner, Victor. *The Anthropology of Performance.* New York: PAJ Publications, 1986.

Uzoigwe, Joshua and Gary Weltz. "Three Songs." *African Arts* vol.7, No.3, UCLA, 1974.

Uzoigwe, Joshua. "Contemporary Techniques of Composition by African Composers: A Preliminary Investigation." *International Folk Music Newsletter,* Edinburgh, 1978.

_____. "The Problem of Analyzing Traditional Music: Analyzing Ukom Music," *Studies in Traditional Music and Dance,* edited by Peter Cook. Cambridge: University of Edinburgh,1980.

_____. "A Cultural Analysis of Akin Euba's Musical Works." *Odu: Journal of West African Studies,* No.24, 1983.

_____. "Tonal Organisation in Ukom Drum Performance." *Nigerian Magazine* vol.54, No.3, 1986.

_____. "In Conversation with Israel Nwankwo: Igbo Master Musician." *Black Perspective in Music* vol.14, No.2, 1986.

_____. **"Operational and Hierachical Forms of Creativity in Igbo Music: The Ukom Music as a Case Study."** *Ife: Annals of the Institute of Cultural Studies,* No. 2, 1988.

_____. "Nigerian Composers and their Works." *Daily Times,* 25 August and 1 September 1990.

_____. **"African Drum Technique: The Case of Igbo Master Players."** *Journal of the Center for Black African Civilization,* 1992a.

_____. *Akin Euba: An Introduction to the Life and Music of a Nigerian composer.* Bayreuth: Eckhard Breitinger, 1992b.

Vidal, Olatunji. *Traditions and History in Yoruba Music.* In *Nigerian Music Review,* edited by Akin Euba, No.1, 1977.

Recent Articles about Joshua Uzoigwe

Euba, Akin. "Remembering Joshua Uzoigwe: Exponent of African Pianism (1946-2005)." *Journal of the Musical Arts in Africa* 2 (2005): 84-88.

Sadoh, Godwin. "Creativity and Dance in Joshua Uzoigwe's Music." *Composer-USA* 9, No. 2 (2003): 4-5.

_____. "Intercultural Creativity in Joshua Uzoigwe's Music." *Africa* 74, No. 4 (December 2004): 633-661.

_____. "The Creative Experience of a Contemporary Nigerian Composer." *Living Music* 20, No. 1 (Spring 2005): 6-9.

_____. "Hybrid Composition: An Introduction to the Age of Atonality in Nigeria." *The Diapason* 97, No. 11 (November 2006): 22-25.

_____. "Nigerian Art Music Composers." *NTAMA,* January 10, 2007.

_____. "Twentieth Century Nigerian Composers." *Choral Journal* 47, No. 10 (April 2007): 33-39.

About the Author

Godwin Sadoh is a Nigerian ethnomusicologist, composer, church musician, organist, pianist, choral conductor, and publishing scholar. He has a B.A. degree in piano performance from the Obafemi Awolowo University, Nigeria; M.A. in ethnomusicology from the University of Pittsburgh; M.M. in organ performance and church music from the University of Nebraska-Lincoln; and in May 2004, Sadoh received the Doctor of Musical Arts degree in organ performance and composition from Louisiana State University, Baton Rouge; making him the first African to earn a doctoral degree in organ performance from any institution in the world. Sadoh's thirty-three scholarly articles on Nigerian church music, organ building, composers, modern African art music, African musicology and intercultural musicology is published in notable journals in America, Canada and Europe, including The Hymn, The Diapason, The Organ, Choral journal, Composer-USA, Africa, Living Music, Organ Encyclopedia, Percussive Notes, NTAMA, and the Contemporary African Database. He is the author of several books, including E Korin S'Oluwa: Fifty Indigenous Christian Hymns from Nigeria (2005); Twenty-five Preludes on Yoruba Church Hymns (2006); Intercultural Dimensions in Ayo Bankole's Music (2007); and The Organ Works of Fela Sowande: Cultural Perspectives (2007). Sadoh has taught at several institutions of higher learning such as the Obafemi Awolowo University, University of Pittsburgh, University of Nebraska-Lincoln, Thiel College in Pennsylvania State, Golden West College, California, Baton Rouge College, LeMoyne-Owen College, Tennessee, and Talladega College, Alabama. Courses taught include Music of Africa, History of American Jazz, World Music, Music Appreciation, Sacred Music courses, Theory of Music, Form and Analysis, Counterpoint, History of Music, Choral Conducting, Choral Literature, Composition, Piano, Organ, and Voice. He has concertized as a recitalist, accompanist, and choral conductor all over Nigeria and the United States. And he also served as Organist and Choir Director at numerous churches in Nigeria as well as the United States. Sadoh has composed for all the music media–organ, piano, vocal solo, choral, electronic, chamber and the orchestra. His music has been performed and recorded at various colleges and universities, churches, radio and television stations in Canada, Costa Rica, Germany, Great Britain, Italy, Luxembourg, Nigeria, Norway, and the United States. Sadoh is a recipient of the prestigious ASCAPLUS Award for four years in a row in recognition of the publications and performances of his compositions world wide. His biography is listed in Marquis Who's Who in America, Who's Who in American Education, Who's Who in the World and the Contemporary African Database, London. Wayne Leupold Editions, Evensong Music, and Wehr's Music House are the publishers of Sadoh's compositions. Sadoh was appointed Assistant Professor of Music and Director of the Sacred Music Program at LeMoyne-Owen College, Memphis, Tennessee, in fall 2005. And he was appointed to the position of Full Professor of Music at Talladega College, Alabama in fall 2007.